(L)Agent of Justice
Season 2

Table of Contents

Previosly on Last Season

"…He once had his foster mother got murdered and has lived alone ever since."
"What about his biological family?" he asked.

"My name is Specter. I was sent by your father to assist your investigation." he said as he took off his hat. I remain silent until he put his hat back on and lit his cigarette.

"You look good," he greeted me.
"I'm better than looking good." I just realized that the person next to me is my father.
"This is time when you and I talk."

"No shake hands," he said, getting up from the chair. I reflexively see my empty hand that doesn't shake hands with his.
"It only with a hug," he said hugging me. I just hug him back. A moment later he returns to sit on the chair and I follow him. Suddenly his face is not as stiff as before. He is more relaxed and less formal.
"Ha ha ha...! You're still the same, always serious," he said patting my shoulder making me almost spit out the drink I am sipping.

"May I know which institution you are from, gentlemen?" I asked and he handed me his business card that said 'private detective'.
"It is a pleasure to make you an acquaintance, Mr. West."

"Thanks for helping me."
"I still have things to say, young master," I paused and waited for what he wanted to say.
"I've been reassignment. Perhaps you will get other agents to help you."
"So this is a goodbye." Specter got up and opened the door to leave, but he held back as if he wanted to say something.
"What you will see next is more dangerous than you think." Specter immediately left me.

CASE 1 – Scandal of Celebrities

It's been half a year since the case at the Wall Office, I'm starting to live the relaxed days of my career. I admit that the drastic changes that occurred earlier were not the changes I was expecting, but fortunately everything was still fine. I think I missed the time when it was fighting criminals that tried to hurt innocent people. But that feeling of longing cannot be offset by the loss of Specter, a partner, as well as a member of my father's secret agent, who was assigned to support and even protect me, more precisely we fought side by side. Right now I can't find him at all. Even I tried to meet him at Arandre Bar but he never came.

I'm currently carrying out my usual activities in my office, busy giving lots of marks to the samples I've researched. This job went on smoothly and agilely that I then typed my report.

"Grant, all conditions on the victim found no irregularities," said a woman whose desk was across from me.

"Try to check the exon level."

"Protein and amino acid levels, good point, thank you." The woman started running the test from the instructions I gave her.

Meet Caith Winter, a biochemist. I asked Captain Briggs to let a biochemist work as a forensic partner. Honestly, I really need the presence of someone who can help me to run the test and not have to go back and forth from the filed to the office until the results are out.

"I think you're right, Grant."

"The results are out?" I approached Caith's desk and understood the results of the test he was taking. Suddenly a knock on the door startled us.

"Hey, are you guys busy?"

"We're okay. What's wrong, Inspector?" Eddie entered our room.

"Can you come with me?" I saw Caith who was still taking notes on her work.

"It's okay, Grant. You guys have fun."

"I'll be back to help with your work."

"I'm fine Grant. Good luck." I went to follow Eddie and we got in the car and drove towards the crime scene.

"So, what are we dealing with this time?"

"A kidnapping."

"Any demands?"

"We will hear directly from the family." The car continues to go to the elite housing in Bratginia 'World Palace'. This housing is occupied by many rich people who work as bank directors, entrepreneurs, successful artists, and other figures. This case has continued with the kidnapping of 3 famous people. I didn't think that there was another important person in Bratginia to be victim of this kidnapping.

When we arrive at the Gold block no. 41. A magnificent house with an area of approximately 50 square meters and the size of a 3-level house decorated with clean white paint. Four police cars stand guard outside its 250 centimetres tall fence and two police cars park at its doorstep. We enter the courtyard of the victim's house after being checked by the guard in front of the house.

"This is so amazing," I said admiring the whole yard which was decorated with lots of flowers and carved statues with fountains.

"Focus, Grant! After all this case involves famous people then the impact on us will also be bigger."

"My mind is calm and ready to work." Before we enter the door. A distant shout called out to me. We turn to see who was calling us. It turns out that was Rip, who was late, was being escorted by one of the house keepers using a golf cart.

"Thank goodness I am on time."

"Come in!" Eddie ushered us in and was greeted by the butler of the house named Alphonse. Eddie flashed his police badge and the house's butler welcomed us to follow him to the landlord. We enter the large living room and see a landlord comforting a woman who I thought is his wife.

"Mr Calvin, an inspector would like to see you." the man rose from his seat and greeted us.

"Eddie Monrow - detective."

"Merrick Calvin. Thank you for coming so quickly."

"Glad to help you, Mr Calvin." He invited us to sit on the sofa. I chose to remain standing and look around. Rip didn't seem to hesitate to follow Eddie to sit on a comfortable couch.

"Can you tell us how it happened?"

"Two days ago, our son, Hadyn, was worried that someone was following him. Of course we tightened our guard to protected him then. However, last night he did not come home and his cellphone could not be reached."

"Any demands from the kidnapper?"

"Trust me inspector, if he wants money from us we will get him out. Unfortunately nothing at all, no asking for ransom."

"Could it be... my son has..." The woman next to him was sobbing hysterically remembering the sentence in her mind was that her child had died.

"Calm down ma'am, we can't be sure until we find your son."

"Is there anything you could give us, Inspector?"

"We have tracked in the last eight hours found no information about traffic accidents or eyewitnesses who saw the kidnapping incident."

"Can you find him, sir?"

"We will do our best, for the time being what you have to do is to wait for our news or let us know if the kidnapper contacts you." Eddie rose from his seat and shook hands with Mr. Calvin.

"Has someone recently break in your home?" Eddie turned to me and the expressions on the faces of the two owners seemed to be hiding something from us.

"How can you say that?"

"I didn't say but your desk has traces of things that was there before but now is gone." I showed him a table with a thin white square-shaped outline imprinted on its glistening brown luxurious wooden table.

"In case you forgot, before we entered this house. I saw that the surveillance camera leading to the front door was broken and had marks of something hitting your porch floor. I assume it was this thing that was slammed." Eddie looked back at Mr. calvin. He seemed to be holding back from speaking.

"This has nothing to do with the kidnapping of our child," said Mrs. Calvin quick. I just avert my eyes and kept looking at the mark like a miniature statue.

"That thing is a sculpture of my face that I got from a film world award."

"Can we have a look at your son's room?" Their expressions were getting erratic with my spontaneous behavior to check on them.

"Forgive us, Mr. and Mrs. Calvin. It is very important for us to get a lead about your child." Mr. Calvin quickly relented with my wishes while his wife just gave in to her husband's wishes. We are escort by Calvin couple and Eddie quickly comes over and whispers to me.

"You're a profiler now?"

"No, but are you sure you can find it without knowing what kind of person it is?"

"You can?"

"We will see.' We've reached the second floor and the first three rooms to the right are Hadyn's.

"Please." Mr. Calvin ushered us into the room and I immediately take a look at what was in the room. Eddie and Rip who don't know what I am doing are just nervous when they see me looking at everything in the room. I see the arrangement of books, trophies, the contents of his study table, and the telescope by the window.

"Your son, he's amazing."

"Did you find anything?"

"Before I answer that, Inspector, did your son by any chance join the scientific work community at his school or similar?"

"We only know he joined the astrology community at his school."

"I don't think so."

"What do you mean, Grant?"

"Judging from his book collection, he's taken up some political science recently."

"Impossible. He is only 19 years old."

3

"And a plan that he laid out on this wall. He seems to mark major foreign political cases." I showed them the world map that was taped right above his desk with some information that I wasn't too familiar with to hear the history of it. I explained one by one the political conflicts from previous 200 years which he tried to relate to several political cases that tended to increase in this country, namely the corruption of the state leadership.

"Did he clean up his room himself?"

"No Mr. Grant, we have a maid cleaning the room."

"That means something might be left here," I tried to sniff out a scent that seemed familiar to me. I open the window and check the outside edges and found a burn mark on the lower end of the window which had been dragging against the floor.

"These burn marks... like cigarette butts."

"He doesn't smoke!" firm Mrs. Calvin.

"If it's not him then the person who snuck in here managed to get in through his room." I came out of the room and the look on Mr. Calvin seemed to expect me to find a clue.

"I have several possible locations that know where he is. Let us work." I left them followed by Rip. Eddie seems to apologize to the couple for my possibly offending behavior and follows me out of the house.

"Okay. As for theft, how did you know?"

"You can see it." I pointed at the camera oversight and a crack in the terrace floor as I described earlier.

"How can you see it?"

"Detective, I don't think I need to explain everything to you."

"I will regret it if I hear you insult me. Nice move." We got into the car and left the mansion. Our journey, which still has no direction, is accompanied by Rip, who is busy fiddling with his laptop.

"You got their footage?"

"Only at the time of the incident did we lose the tape at the front door. The culprit fired his pistol with a silencer."

"Another angle? He couldn't have been there all of a sudden."

"I've seen it, there's nothing coming." Rip handed me his laptop for me to check one more time.

"Any possible for inside work?"

"Of course not. Rip skipped Hadyn's part of the room."

"What? Impossible." Rip peeked from the back seat to see what he had missed.

"You saw this the night before the culprit tampered with the footage, nothing strange happened to the footage that led to Hadyn's room."

"I told you so."

"However, you didn't realize that ten minutes before the front door's camera went off, there was a fairly strong gust of wind blowing outside the house."

"So?"

4

"You see how the footage guarding Hadyn's room?"

"There is no wind there."

"Because it is a pre-recorded loop."

"The tapes have been tampered."

"That's how the intruder got in."

"Didn't any of the guards see it?"

"Let's assume the intruders have gathered information and got the guard protocol at the house."

"Fair enough."

"Any ideas about the missing child?"

"I have one or two. Turn right here Inspector." Eddie turned his car around surprised at my direction.

"Please explain to us."

"The kid gets involved with people who happen to be at the group meeting."

"One of the gathering places is 'Freedom' right?" Eddie parked his car near a brick-colored building.

"One of three groups of people protesting state policy."

"Are we safe going in there?" Rip hesitated to enter the area filled with anarchists.

"Do you want to come?" asked Eddie offering to Rip.

"You're fine here alone."

"Good idea, thanks, mate."

"Please keep an eye on this area. If anything happened call us on intercom." Eddie and I left the car and entered the building where a gathering of people exchanged ideas about state politics.

"Secure channel 5." Rip's voice came into our comms.

"Channel 5, secured." I replied.

"By the way, how do you know there are cigarette marks. The room was cleaned every day.

"Everyone is lazy about something. Even the maid doesn't check every job until it's finished."

"And you can smell it because?"

"Wind blows, Inspector. Cigarette burnt marks will still be there apart from being cleaned."

"Why didn't he kidnap him when he was still at home?"

"He needed something in that child. Kidnapping him at home risks getting caught when trying to escape."

We walk through room after room and we are face with a large door. I see people having discussions and some reading newspapers. I feel like I'm in another world with some activity talking about a news that is broadcast. There are also those who are arguing with the strength of a balanced opinion so that one does not want to budge. In the midst of the din of a room someone greeted us from the front door.

"Good afternoon, are you here to join this community?"

"I think we pass for the offer. Do you run this place?"

"Yes, my name is Reeche. The only one running this place. You are?"

"I'm a police inspector from Ruchester PD and this is my associate, Dylan, we'd like to ask you a question. Can we find a comfortable place to talk?" Eddie turned to leave the room, but Reeche folded his arms refusing to follow Eddie.

"Why? So you can take me without people around here knowing?" he said sarcastically.

"We'd like to ask you a few questions if you don't mind."

"Yeah, and ended up in prison. I know exactly how 'speaking elsewhere' works in this crowd." He raised his voice so that many people were distracted by us at the door. I am the one who was still calm between Eddie who was still defending himself from Reeche's directionless shouts. I interrupt them by giving Reeche a hand gesture to stop him yelling.

"What's your problem, sir?"

"What do you mean?"

"We were just standing here, wanting to ask you a thing or two and you refused by trying to provoke us."

"I've had bad experiences with the authorities."

"As far as you're concerned, we didn't do anything to you." The situation began to cool off and began to calm down. I motioned to Eddie to just start asking questions here and Eddie pulled out a photo.

"Are you familiar with this kid?"

"Is that Hadyn? Has something happened to him?"

"His parents informed us that he didn't come home last night."

"So this is all about Hadyn."

6

"Was he here yesterday?"

"Yes. He is here."

"Until what time?"

"As far as I know until 9:00 p.m. it might be little bit more."

"Did he come home alone?" Reeche thought hard to remember last night's events.

"He's with Nate." Someone helped Reeche to remember.

"Ah yes. Nate was with him when he came home."

"Is he here?"

"Not yet, community activities usually start from 17.00 to 19.00, this place is open until 22.00."

"Looks like we'll be waiting for him to come here. Can you contact us when he arrives?" Eddie handed Reeche his name card.

"Feel free to join us when we ask him questions." We left him and with a soft beat of his voice. It was Reeche who called out to us.

"E-excuse me."

"Anything else?"

"It seems we have a misunderstanding from each other's point of view and your words have opened my eyes. I hope we can make a fresh start." I nudged Eddie to shake his hand.

"Don't worry about it, you're a good guy."

"I'll call when I find Nate." We once again left the room and Eddie's relief of interaction with the group Eddie was worried about was over.

"We can get through it pretty smoothly for now."

"Do you want to rest or go to the next place?"

"I'm not that old, I don't want to be left behind by you."

"That's the spirit, Inspector." We entered the car and immediately left.

"How was it?" Rip asked.

"Very smooth thanks to this champ." Eddie spilled his success on me.

"Anything wrong around here?" I changed the subject.

"There isn't any. I'm almost bored waiting."

"Looks like we're done here."

"We'll be waiting at forces." Eddie drove his car and took us back to the police force.

Arrived at headquarters Tess waited for her father to have lunch. He don't forget to invite me, but I refused because I still had work to do. I promised him to do another day. They left and I meet Caith when I reached the third floor.

"How was the investigation?"

"We are still waiting for someone to question."

"I feel grateful that you came back at this hour."

"Why is that?" We entered our office and I saw that there were many dishes on Caith's table.

"You look happy, Caith."

"Sorry, looks like I bought too much. May I share it with you?"

"Sure, why not?"

"Looks like we need extra hand to eat it." I shifted my chair and looked at the pile of food that seemed too much even for the two of us.

"I've thought about it, don't worry."

"Hey Caith."

"Hey, come in and join us for lunch."

"Do you mind, Grant?" Rip asked while walking slowly towards us.

"She's the boss." Caith smiled and gave a chair to Rip. Caith shared her food with us and I also helped distribute drinks for them.

"How's work, Rip?"

"I am just sightseeing. He is the one who does most of the work." I also just laughed at Rip's answer.

"I have my own role, and so do you."

"I'm just running away from scary stuff, Grant, but you're different." Once again Rip weighed himself against me.

"Is it true?" Caith was curious about what was happening on the field.

"You should have seen him when he was chasing criminals in Wall Office."

"It is nothing." I humbled.

"But you're the one behind them, right?"

"I'm just a comm guy."

"That's good, isn't it?" hearing Caith Rip's response smiled to himself.

"Nice move," I whispered to Rip who was trying to win over Caith. The conversation took place while finishing the food that Caith bought. Rip helped to finish her food. After lunch, I helped tidy up the room and we returned to our posts.

"Thank you Grant. It turns out that you can work very well with Rip."

"He's a nice guy with a special set of skill."

"See… here is the result of my trial report." Caith gave me the report.

"Nice job, Caith. You saved me today."

"With this, you only need to give the report on to Captain Briggs. You can focus back on your case right?"

"This is amazing. See you later." I rushed to Captain Briggs and presented my report. I'm not forget to mention Caith who contributed greatly to the completion of this report. Before I left the room, captain stopped me.

"Good work, Grant."

"No Captain, as I said. Caith did it."

"But, you are capable of emerging one's talents. You become a leader in your own way."

"Did something happen captain? You're acting strange," Captain Briggs steadied himself and looked at me intently.

"Has your father in touched with you again after such a long time?"

"Just once, when I least expected it."

"Has he asked you to join his agency?"

"He asked for it and I refused."

"May I ask why?"

"I like it here, sir. I can do a better job here."

"Thank you for your kind words. You may go back to your work."

"Then excuse me, Captain." I left his room full of questions about my father's influence to the force. I hope it doesn't last.

That night Eddie took me to meet Nate, the important person who is the key to Hadyn's disappearance. Reech contacted us and waited for us to arrive at Freedom. Reech, who is waiting for us with Nate, invites us to ask questions to Nate, of course this time the situation is more conducive than before. Me and Eddie feel welcome kindly this doesn't mean we aren't careful when asking Nate. We cross each answer with another question that proves that he answers honestly. Nate admits that he parted ways with Hadyn three blocks from here because someone was picking him up in a luxury car. Hadyn got into the car without anything strange about him and he promised to meet again today.

"Thank you for your time." Eddy finished taking notes.

"Detective, can you help Hadyn?"

"We will follow up on the information you provided, if you have nothing more to say, we will on our way out." We left them and Eddie immediately contacted Rip.

"Rip, black luxury car 3 blocks east."

"Means Hadyn didn't notice that he was taken by a different person." We rushed to catch up with Rip who is still in the office to get a trace of the car that Hadyn had taken.

"We're here, is anything happened?"

"As you all know how I work to follow every camera that its passed. They're still driving around for ten minutes."

"What do you think?" Eddie asked me who was still contemplating their movements from the screen Rip had prepared.

"They walked around in circles to make sure no one was following them."

"How long will they be like that?"

"Or you can fast forward the recording right?" Rip, who had forgotten his equipment, just remembered the idea I gave him.

"Sorry about that," and fast-forwarding from the tape we traced the car's path all the way to Prester.

"We lost them."

"I will conduct further investigations." I left Eddie and Rip then took my phone out of the base. While hailing a taxi to take me somewhere. My hands quickly type short messages and send them. Only fifteen minutes later I arrived at Bar Arandre. I met a face that was familiar to me as a regular at this place which was also a meeting place with a friend.

"Welcome, Mr Grant. You worked late today?"

"Thank you, you look good Andrew."

"Thank you, the bartender is always the best when he stands behind the bar."

"A glass of Old Pal, please."

"Coming right up." While Andrew was preparing the ingredients to make my drink, the bar door opened and someone wearing an all-white suit and the white hat he took off when he entered the bar. The bartender takes his cue for the drink he was about to order and he took a seat right next to me.

"You got something for me, Phil?"

"We found it, young master." My drink was handed over by the bartender along with his order.

"The car stopped at a luxury house in the inner circle of Prester, west zone here to be precise." Phil handed over an envelope with a map sheet which he had marked with satellite photos.

"Has any intelligence seen there?"

"Everything mentioned here is the entertainment venue in Prester. All kinds, you name it."

"The Don's family is smaller than the entire Prester society. Somehow rich people formed this entertainment business and are able to invite people from all level."

"When are we going to start?"

"Finish the drink and let's go."

We leave the bar and use the car that Phil has prepared. The car is moving at a moderate speed which estimate we would arrive by tomorrow morning. While on this trip, I have contacted Don to meet me. As the new ruler of Prester, he has the important business of rebuilding his family. Their main business is automotive and wild racing. The city has been the center of attention for racing maniac since the disappearance of the gang factions. Tonight's drive is accompanied by a story from Phil about the reforms at Prester over the last three months. Their competition is no longer in the power of the mafia, but in the business class where the only people who can survive are those who can circulate cash. It is still unknown who, but many new players appear who are trying to replace Don in controlling Prester again. I sensed that Don's rise in possession still had the ripples of the groups trying to compete. They form groups by making money and that money is used to strengthen their group. So far there has been no conflict between these groups, but that doesn't mean it can't arise suddenly.

"Okay thank you." I closed my cell phone and closed my reading of Prester. Phill's car was getting closer to Prester as the sun rose.

We have to pass through the outer circle before entering the inner circle. I will never forget the sight of seeing this zone as a slum, but in contrast to the zone in the middle which looks grand and luxurious and full of facilities. Phil drives his car faster so you can get to the inner circle quicker. Phil stopped the car at a large garage building with lots of garages which made me wonder what they are doing inside. The atmosphere is quite lively, the workers make their car according to the taste of the customer, both in terms of paint, body shape, engine type, and even accessories. We entered through the door of what I assumed was their office and a man with dreadlocks hair got up from the table and puffed on a cigar trying to greet a potential customer.

"Welcome, gentlemen, how can we help you at the workshop?"

"Well that depends on how much you can spare for our car," I pointed at Phil's car which was parked outside.

"Are there any special specifications? Accessories? Bumper? Spoilers? Rims?"

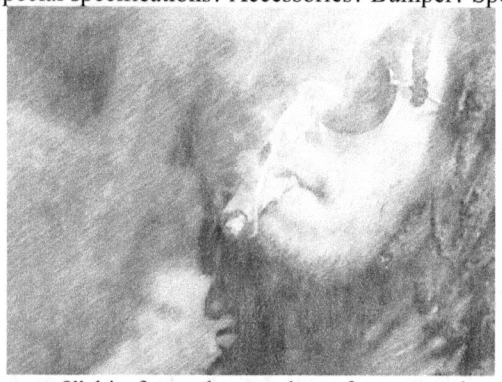

'How about weapons?" his formerly merchant face started to show a serious frown on hisself assuming this prospect of his could be their enemy. Then the look on his face trying to hold my bluff.

"Don't joke like that, sir, we don't sell any weapons here."

"Is that true? I'm sure the person standing across the street also knows what I want."

"If you don't want to buy anything, I suggest leave this place at once!" came many people from the front door we entered and I knew very well whose footsteps those were.

"Who's going to left this place?"

"Ah, welcome back, father! These gentlemen want to leave because they didn't buy anything."

"They are my guests."

"They..." the greeter was silent and we followed Don's direction to walk towards the door which was not visible because it was painted black according to the color of the workshop.

"Basement, again? What's wrong with you with basements?" Don just kept silent and continued to walk towards an iron door in front of him.

"Watch your head!" Don pointed at the ceiling at the narrowing staircase before entering his room.

"This time the place is more appropriate."

"Now we don't have to relocate anymore. You could say this is more worthy." He sat in his chair and I sat facing him while Phill chose to stay standing behind me.

"What can I help you with this time?" I handed Don's men a folder of photographs to give to him. Don looked at it carefully, especially at the part of the car which he thought really caught his eye.

"I guess I'm familiar with this car."

"How could that be?"

"A Logo on the vehicle." I approached him and tried to pay attention to the logo that Don was referring to.

"What logo is this?"

"New mega casino 'Cleopatra'"

"Then we will go there," I said in a hurry to leave this basement.

"Wait, young master!" Phill stops me before I leave them.

"The reason they built a gambling holy land in this city is because they were able to form small gangsters who have massive cash flow."

"We don't know who they are or how to kidnap those people."

"We will check them one by one."

"That place is too wide for two people to inspect." Don gave me his clue.

"We can't keep everyone inside because the place is also being visited by VIPs who might just be your superiors.

"Okay, I'll just drop by there."

"I'll take you to shopping around."

"One more thing Mr Wade, we don't participate in reconnaissance, only when needed."

"I'm well aware of that. See you. Thank you for the help." We left Don's base and looked for proper clothes to join in the casino.

We arrive at Cleopatra. The luxury that gets tonight is enlivened by many celebrities and wealthy people. Phil gave us access by registering with reception. Entering this building is no less bright than the lights they exhibit outside the casino. The hustle and bustle of the game where their money is at stake is followed by excitement and joy. Various kinds of games presented by the host. Amazing I think they manage this kind of thing. But I'm not here as a policeman trying to catch this gambling activity, but as a citizen who is concerned about the kidnapping victims.

"What are we going to look for?"

"We split up, cover more ground about the kidnapped people." We split up to look around. A place this large would take some time to find the right clue. Several games I've passed there is nothing strange with this place. Losing players leave and replace with new ones. Likewise with players who win, he goes to exchange his winnings for some money.

One hour I'm going around once looking around, Phill called me through the communication device.

"Young master."

"You got something?"

"Sounds like a waste of time. This place is nothing but disguise."

"I think so. We're out of here!" We headed for the main door to leave this place. The visitors keep showing up and are very excited to visit this place. Someone approached us when we wanted to open the exit.

"Gentlemen, why do you guys leaving?"

"We've gambled enough. It's time to leave."

"But we are here to provide loan facilities for people who want to get their money back," hearing that, Phil and I felt odd about this place.

"What do you mean by loan?"

"Ah... looks like the gentlemen are the new visitors." He explained to us in a friendly manner some of the assistance offered by the casino owners.

"What happens to those who fail to pay?"

"The host will take whatever is equal to the amount owed."

"Thank You. We'll be more careful," we immediately left the place and tried to observe from outside the casino area. We headed for the car that Phill had prepared to park outside

"Phill assure me, how many people have been reported mysteriously missing?"

"Three of the famous family, but too many to count for common folks."

"They don't report to the police because they are afraid of the amount of debt they have." Phill is busy accessing data from his car which is equipped with sophisticated equipment to get information. Some files had been sent to him and he showed them to me.

"This is not possible."

"This case is more dangerous than we thought. Young master better step down, let us handle this."

"Me? Back off?" I said to myself. I remembered my ability is better than this.

"Excuse me..." A man's voice tried to call out to us amidst the seriousness of the case. I remember his voice. Someone I don't expect is here.

"Mr. West, what a surprising coincidence." I got out of the car and greeted them both.

"We saw you as you were getting in the car and I thought I'd like to report something..." The private detective paused as he saw Phil getting out of the car.

"I don't remember you. You have a different partner this time."

"Well, since I knew this case would be impossible to solve by being a 'cop', So I used a different approach."

"Independent agents, interesting."

"And you called me because?"

"Ah... we happened to be here because someone directed us and didn't know that this place was a casino."

"You're looking for a missing person?"

"Lots. Everyone in this photo has mysteriously disappeared." Mr. West handed me his cell phone and showed me the screen with the face of someone I didn't recognize at all and many others showing up to 30 people.

"How did you trace your investigation to here?"

"How about you first?"

"I did not disclose the police investigation."

"But you're not a cop, not tonight." I was speechless, he was not cooperative at all and I tried to calm down.

"We tracked using surveillance cameras and satellites on a car that kidnapped this child. We followed his movements all the way here…"

"Using a satellite camera only powerful people can do it, it suits you..."

"Brother." I was surprised that Phill said the same words as Mr. West. What a surprising coincidence that these brothers met in the same case.

"I guess you still like being a private detective, running around with your sniffing nose looking for mysteries."

"How does your majesty shoe feel? Still shinny?"

"Still acting like a child, grow up!"

"Like you?"

"Surrounded by people who admire your intelligence, feel their admiration, not for fame, not for wealth."

"Money and fame are not my thing."

"I work hard for my life. So you have to get it for you."

"Do you have a happy life, dear brother?" Phill was silent for a moment and chuckled at his brother's words.

"Why do you care if success makes me happy or not?" Mr. West, who initially spoke without looking at Phil, quickly looked at his brother's face.

"Exactly, why would anyone care?" he approached and looked firmly into Phill's eyes to confirm the answer himself. Then he turned away from him again.

"I have a good life."

"Are you sure about that?" John's question made Phil speechless holding back his anger.

"The family reunion doesn't seem to be going well, can we get back to matters?" I tried to stop the arguing between the brothers until they calmed down and John told me the results of his investigation.

"According to our investigation, this missing person was abducted and used as a trial for a new drug."

"What kind of drugs?"

"Kind of narcotics."

"Where are these people now?"

"Half of them are in the outer circle zone in critical condition due to an overdose."

"My God."

"The ambulance has taken them. We hope they are safe."

"Looks like we'll have to check this place out one more time, now we know what we're looking for."

"For this rare opportunity I'm offering a partner combination." Phill gave Mr. West and his partner.

"Just so you know that I don't want to be with you, dear brother."

"I will work with him instead, dr. Ernest I'm believe." Phil pointed at Mr. West' friend to be his investigative partner.

"And my dear brother will going along with young master."

"Young master?"

"Long story."

"I look forward to it."

"With this we all agree." me and Mr. West moves to the heart of the case.

"I think we should reconsider this." Dr. Ernest who doesn't seem to really agree with the selection of this partner. We enter Cleopatra again. It's like repeating the incident when it started when we entered a building full of exuberance by bettors of wealth, while we have to find out where the source of this drug distribution is.

"Let's split up once more, this time we know what we're looking for."

Me and Mr. West are looking for new clues together starting from the east side, while Phill and Dr. Ernest are going to the west side.

"Mr. West."

"Just John, please."

"All right, John. So, how long have you been a private investigator? How does it feel?"

"10 years, very delightful so far," he replies quickly and I get the feeling he doesn't really like to chat while working. I'm trying to focus more with my observations here.

"And you sir, you turn out to be a royal family, right?"

"It's hard to say a member of the family if my father never saw me when I was a kid."

"Did he tell you why?"

"I would loved to tell you that if I asked him." I chuckled imagining what dad would say if I asked this.

"So, tough love?"

"Not really. I was lived at the 'House of Hanny'"

"That famous Hanny orphanage?"

"May God bless his soul, yes it is, John."

"I heard there was a tragedy there."

"Huh? So you started your career as a kid."

"I was only an eleven year old boy at the time. Glanced over the news and tried to contact the Ruchester PD for follow up on the case but no one heard me."

"Thank you, I appreciate it." John suddenly stopped and I followed what he saw,

"Did you accept that before?"
"I wasn't sure to see it when I first came in."

****

"So you are his brother?" Phill only hear dr. Earnest question.
"How could I never heard this?"
"John doesn't always like to talk about his family."
"Did you guys fight?"
"You saw how it was when we met each other."
"I can't imagine if you two in christmas day."
"And you dr. Ernest is a retired combat medic, why not live in one of the many houses in Bratginia?"
"I'm sorry if I said it's none of your business."
"You have guts doctor."
"What do you want?"
"I want to give you something, dr. Ernest." Phill handed Ernest a brown envelope and he opened it.
"What's this?"
"Think of it as an incentive."
"To do what?"
"Information. Nothing in particular, nothing that makes you feel uncomfortable, just let me know what he's doing." Dr. Ernest was silent and Phill's expression changed at what he saw.
"What is it?" Phill just pointed with his face at something.
"Welcome cake, sir?" A woman offers pastries to welcome guests, Phill refuses by shaking his head.
"Thank You." Dr. Ernest took it. Phill watches the woman leave them and immediately disappeared from the crowd and then Phill slapped dr. Ernest hand who wants to eat the welcome cake.
"Don't you dare eat that!"
"Huh? Why?" Phill handed over the airtight plastic bag and took the cake from dr. Ernest then seals and saves it. He tucks into his jacket worriedly, but the casino lights suddenly went out. In the midst of the darkness that confused the four of us. Faint silence guests who previously were rejoicing as if waiting for something.

The lights were shining on the north side and someone was wearing a dress that flashed brightly reflecting off the lights. All the visitors cheered again and approached the stage on the north side. We followed the crowd slowly so that we were at the very back to see the figure of a man holding a microphone standing on the stage.

"Welcome to Cleopatra!" greeted the man while followed by the cheers of the audience received his speech.

"You guys like the outcome of the bet?!" The audience cheered to welcome the host passionately.

"I'm just saying hello to all the loyal casino diners, we'll be back soon. Enjoy everything in this place, we have a great bar, restaurant and every betting game!"

"Let's bet, live, and be happy!!" his roaring roar revived the cheers of the guests and the casino lights were back on. They all returned to their respective games and activities began again.

"Who is he?", my voice goes into the com and startles Phill and dr. Ernest.

"Grand Vintage, owner and manager of this place." said Phill.

"If we want to find an answer out of this case. He's the man we need."

"Calm down young master, you can't approach him that easily."

"I don't know about that. Me and John are looking for him."

"Where are you now, young master?" My voice starts to cut off turning off the communication device.

"Looks like they turned off the communication device."

"Bollocks!!" In the midst of Phill's panic now, John and I made our way down the backstage aisle after turning off the comms.

"Feels good."

"You look excited."

"Nothing has ever been more exciting than knowing my brother is panicking and a dangerous case."

"Any chance we get out of here alive?"

"I'm not gambling, Grant, I live on it," hearing him look excited, I also have to follow his spirit.

Phill immediately returned to his car and sent the cake through his agent.

"I need the results as soon as possible!" His subordinates immediately worked on his car and Phil opened the trunk of his car.

"Think again, Phil. We won't be able to just walk in with all this weapon."

"I'm not going to sit idly by and wait until this is over, dr. Ernest."

"We'll go in after the undercover agents start a move in there."

"They're on standby there?""

"Exactly right. Undercover cops will come and they will act from the inside. That's where we come in, now dr. Ernest, choose your weapon wisely."

"Err..." dr. Ernest picked up a revolver and checked the magazine's contents.

"Wise choice dr. Ernest, I hope your aim is not rusty due to your retirement."

"I'm confident of my marksmanship." Phill handed him a magazine.

"Just in case, Doctor."

"Sir, we found it!" Phill was finally informed that the contents of this cake contained narcotics but not ordinary narcotics but five times more effective so that those who ate them would be addicted and be in the casino eternally. Without hearing anything else, Phil immediately headed back to the casino and asked Ernest to message John about what they knew.

"This is not make sense. Why are people coming here more and more if they're going to be cooped up?"

"Because..," answered Phil who was cut off and now moving where John and I are still looking for a way to find Grand Vintage.

"...only a small dose was in the cake. Casinos are open from 10pm to 4am, so there's a full 6 hours they are exposed inside." I explained.

"Very good, why?" John asked.

"They want more victims. If they can go home, no one will notice that they were given drugs and as a bonus they can advertise this place to people they meet."

"Hell always advertises itself is heaven, fantastic!"

"Are you sure we're in the right direction?"

"Of course." John hid himself who almost saw Grand Vintage about to enter his private room. We took a peek at him and confirmed that he actually got into it and tried to eavesdrop on the conversation.

"Playtime is over!" Someone was pointing a gun from behind me and I realized then so was John.

"Looks like we were both caught at once." We were taken by a bodyguard into the Vintage room.

"Mr. Vintage, we caught two suspicious intruders," we were pushed into Vintage's private room at their gunpoint.

"My, my, my.. what a pleasant surprise."

"I think we're happy to surprise you," John's arrogant words made him point a gun right at his head. Vintage gestured for his men to check John and he took a wallet. Vintage takes John's ID card.

"Private detective, hmm... I've seen you in the newspapers."

"Look how the mighty has fallen!" Again, Vintage's men checked and took my wallet this time.

"Who are you? I never heard of you."

"I'm just an ordinary person following him."

"Aagh!" John was hit in the abdomen and I tried to stop him even though they also pulled me.

"I don't like your answer."

"I just followed him." Again John was hit on the same side. Vintage wants to test those of us who try to challenge it.

"I don't have all night. Aim for the head."

"Mr. West, I'll count to three to tell you who's with you or I'll blow your head off."

"Wait! Wait!"

"One!"

"What difference does it make to call him my assistant or the police?"

"Two!"

"Why are you still counting it? I told you already."

"Mr. West, I want to believe in you every second now. Three!"

"No, stop!" Vintage gave a stop signal to his men. I can't say anything about what John will say next.

"He is a secret agent of the Wade family." I was surprised to hear him reveal who I really was, which I also refused to be a part of. Of course this made Vintage more sure of John's answer because he confirmed my uncomfortable face.

"Take them to the exaltation hall."

We were led with gunpoint and forced to walk down the hall until we arrived at a room filled with people enjoying their sleep.

"Interesting right?"

"What's going on here?"

"This is where the people who are repaying their debts to me. They can't get out of here, I'm taking the money from their entire fortune and when it's finished we'll sell their organs and throw the rest into the outer line."

Back to when me and John parted away from Phill, dr. Ernest got part of Phill's understanding of this casino.

"What a terrible plan for this narcotics operation."

"Therefore, dr. Ernest. We must end this place, now!" A group of police cars surrounded the place. Phill signaled his subordinate inside to act by his comms.

"Everybody get down!" shouted many people using firearms to stop gambling activities here. Phill enters the casino with a string of fake cops under the guise of his agents coming in and sees that the casino security is trying to mutiny.

"Drop your weapons!" neither side wants to give in. Phill showed his identity as the head of the police and made this place in the alleged biohazard gas leak, for people who try to resist will not hesitate to be killed on the spot. Hearing that, the casino guards began to drop their weapons and follow the police and the guests. They won't be caught, just keep people safe from being exposed to the noxious gas. The evacuation lasted for an hour and eventually everyone was out of the casino.

"Disperse them and the rest come with me to check all these places."

"Come on, John, where are you?" muttered Phil worried about his brother.

A bodyguard whispers to Vintage informing him of a break-up at the casino.

"Outrageous! Tie them here and we will hit them back!" We were forced to lie down on lounge chairs and tied up as tightly as we could. Not forgetting that they installed a respirator that forced our lungs to inhale the drug. I'm trying not to panic because they've left us here. They tied me pretty tight and I couldn't hold my breath any longer. The shock in my lungs made me gasp for the drug-filled breath. The substance makes my eyes even blurrier and it's hard to remember what I should be doing now. One eye that was still open that glanced at the person died next to me made my brain cells mention the danger I was in. I tried to take the opportunity to calm down and take deep breaths with my calm mind. The seconds the substance tried to eat away at my mind again, I tried to use this opportunity to free myself.

"Hey, don't move!" Vintage Guards opened fire on members of the Phill who were disguised as police. They ran upstairs.

"Don't let them off the hook!" Phill orders his members to return fire. They escape using two helicopters.

"Phill, I can't find them."

"They are tough people, but I'm not sure if they were given that drug."

"Looks like we only have a little time with a few members."

"Sir!!" Phill and Ernest immediately chased towards the sound. They entrusted their agents to go after Vintage. They found the door we were in and there was a kick from the inside.

"Whoever is inside, I will blow this door open!" The banging faded away, but Phill had trouble hearing anyone from inside.

"If you understand my words, get away from the door immediately!" a piece of paper sticking out from the gap under the door. Dr. Ernest realized it was a paper from John's notebook. It says "Mask on!" Phill immediately took his equipment. They had their masks on standby and Phill blew up the door with the pocket bomb he always carried with him.

A plume of smoke billowed out of the door after being blown up. Not only the smoke from the explosion of the pocket bomb but the smoke from the drugs that evaporated in this particular room also came out.

"John!! Young master!"

"We're fine '-John coughed'." "-help them immediately!!"

"There are dozens more like this." I explained with a cough that I was only able to get one person out of this place. Phill quickly asked for medical assistance that had arrived and other officers who were still outside to come in and put on air masks.

"You all right, John?"

"You're a doctor for God's sake... can't you see? ugh.."

"Okay, still annoying. I got you."

"Where's Vintage?"

"He ran away. Come on, forget about him."

"No...Phill, I know where they are."

Vintage's two helicopters are still on the run from their paradise which is currently under siege. He is still annoys by the disturbance he got tonight and tried to start over from what he had elsewhere.

"Hey, are we still being chased?"

"No sir, no signs of pursuers from the ground or the air."

"Very good! Quickly get this helicopter to my jet!" the two helicopters landed immediately at an airport located on the Bratginia airstrip. The helicopter had not yet stopped completely, Vintage immediately ran towards his private jet followed by his bodyguards.

"Hey, where's the pilot?" The escorts who were busy completing the first flight procedures were overwhelmed looking for the pilot who had not yet arrived.

"We're sorry Mr. Vintage, due to a sudden request..."

"Save your excuses, get this plane in the air now!" the pilot had not even finished greeting the owner of the plane. Vintage starts to get riled up with preparations that this long flight will get him caught. The plane starts moving toward the runway. The pilot communicates with air traffic controllers. Suddenly many armed cars and soldiers surrounded them. The plane couldn't avoid them because it was still going very slowly. The siege was over in the blink of an eye. Vintage started to panic and thought that he would do something reckless against the national guard.

"In the name of national security I order this plane to stop! I repeat, stop this plane!" said someone using a loudspeaker. Vintage begins a plan to break through them all, but is surprised by a second warning.

"Get out! Or we blow you out of that plane!"

Vintage was unable to outnumber the national guard. They immediately surrendered and were whisked away from the airport. In the end there was no need for anyone to get hurt.

A few days have passed, a notification from my cellphone rang and it read a message from the commander of the national guard.

"So you called them for help?" said Phill crossing his arms.

"You could say calling the old favor."

"What about the casino?"

"The Don's taking care of it, I think they've looted the place."

"Gangsters! They took advantage when the place was quiet. Many of my members have been injured because of them."

"Only injured, not dead. You should be grateful, dear brother, they did that in their domain." Phill was silent listening to the chatter of his brother and me who were still lying in the hospital. We laugh because we managed to stop Vintage and save the many people who were kidnapped.

"But, you finally found the kid."

"How is he doing, doctor?" i asked.

"Still unconscious, he's under intensive care."

"Grants!" Eddie and Tess came to see me. Her worried face with me lying in the hospital.

"Oh my God, you always make us worry," she said kissing my left hand, which was not attached to an IV.

"Everyone greeted each other, how nice."

"Shut up John!"

"I'm fine. I have partner I can count on." I looked at John who was surprised to hear me.

"I remember you are PE back in Waywell, nice to see you again." Eddie showed his respect.

"Nice to see you too, Inspector, I'm not his friend, by the way." Everyone was shocked except for me who was still smiling.

"John, don't be yourself right now!"

"I like how I am, doctor."

I got up from my bed and tried to walk. Tess and Eddie tried to help the stubborn me to walk.

"You brought what I asked for?"

"I'll bring it for you." Said Tess.

"Take care of him, baby girl."

"I will keep an eye on him." we walked out of my treatment room slowly. Tess who was holding me patiently accompanied me walking towards the room with intensive care patients. I met Mr. and Mrs. calvin. They thanked me for finding their son and I didn't forget to give him a bunch of flowers so he would get well soon. It didn't take long for me to say goodbye to them because my body hurts every inch of it. I lay down again after walking quite far around this hospital.

"Tell me, Grant, how did you guys get on your feet and try to get out of that room full of drug fumes?"
"The explanation is quite simple, doctor, you just don't see it."
"What's that?" John just laughed at Ernest's confusion, who was too honest that he didn't know the effect of drugs to help accelerate the brain for people who are able to control a higher brain capacity or so John said.
"Is that insinuation that you guys are smart or are you really serious?"
"You are the only one doctor in this room, right?" John's joke made our room laugh amidst Ernest's confusion. To be honest I don't know for sure whether what John said is true or not. I feel it myself, I feel invincible. But that's it because the temptation of being unbeatable makes you addicted. So don't use drugs for readers.

Two months passed and I was released from the hospital. I felt my blood flow free from harmful substances and physically my body began to stiffen from lying too long in the hospital. I've started my exercise routine again and this time I'm not going to talk about exercise, but on one occasion I stopped by a place in Bratginia, namely 21B Trisken rd. a neat suit greeted me and invited me to sit on the sofa. His assistant who sat behind him took notes on the discussion I was going to present. He calmly observed me while waiting for my grievance story to consult with him.
"John, I need your help."

===============

CASE 2 – The Nightshade Illusion

Hustle and bustle on Trinsken rd. liven up today's activities. I'm on my way to meet someone to consult about my problem. Yes, to John West, a private investigator. I guess I'll need his services to get the information I want.

I arrived at the door of house number 21B and knocked on the door. A sweet old lady greeted me with her smile.

"Welcome, sir, are you here to see a consultant?"

"Yes, and you are Mrs...?"

"Just call me Celo, the owner of this house."

"Okay, Mrs. Celo, is he here?"

"He is still doing morning activities, come in, it seems you have to wait a while."

"I do not mind." I entered the house with Mrs. Celo and climbed the stairs to the second floor with the noise above.

"Please wait a moment, he's sound little scary like this," whispered Mrs. Celo to me because of the habit of its residents being angry. Mrs. Celo opened the door right after someone from inside the room shouted her name.

"'Hu 'hu... what's wrong boys?" She opened the door and I saw dr. Ernest who is enjoying tea and John who is looking for something.

"Where is it? Where did you keep my stuff?" he said, who was frantically looking for things that I still guessed what he wanted, as well as Mrs. Celo with confused.

"Cigarettes! Where did you put it? What have you done to it?"

"You always tell me to never touch your things."

"I thought you are the housekeeper."

"I'm not." John sighed and saw me standing behind Mrs. Celo.

"Client! I guess you won't even offer me one."

"I don't smoke."

"He's not going to offer it to you John, no one will within two mile radius."

"Grrrhh..." John sounded so desperate.

"Please sit down, Mr. Dylan." Dr. Ernest gave me a chair."

"Let's see from the many things here I want to know how our landlady disappeared recently."

"What do you mean?" Celo confused.

"Look at her already dressed up, you know where she just came from?"

"John." Ernest tried to stop John usual strange behavior.

"You are wearing nice clothes but you can clearly see on her wrist a white sprinkling like flour, right?" I noticed what John was pointing at and it was true.

"Judging from the thickness, it's clearly wheat flour. Meaning, she was just making pizza at the shop next door to Mr. Snow, isn't that right?"

"Come on, what's the point?" John sniffed the scent around him.

"Smells of perfume, wow, you don't only dress attractively, but use perfume too."

"John." Again dr. Ernest tried to stop John with flat voice.

"I advise you not to try to get close to him just because he is a widow. You will be surprised to hear that when he is with Mrs. Wiss who lives across the street travels to tourist spots even people don't know. Well, nobody knows but me."

"John!" Ernest snapped at him.

"I don't know what you're talking about, I don't really know." Mrs. Celo left us in a hurry in tears. I'm sure that behind John's words that might be true hurt her."

"Hah..." he sat down and sighed with satisfaction after channeling anger that was stuck in his head.

"That was very impolite."

"What? Why? She will thank me later."

"Go after her and apologize."

"What? No! you don't want our client waiting here."

"Very busy morning, gentlemen?"

"No, he just needs a case to put his brain to rest." Things were starting to get quieter after the commotion just now. John looked at me expecting that there is an interesting case I would offer him.

"John, I need your help."

"Let me guess, this is about your past, right?" his words hit the spot. To me he was no ordinary private detective. He only used the consultant label, but his abilities are extraordinary.

"It seems you already know what I'm going to say."

"Certainly, from our last meeting it seems you have some curiosity about the ending of that case."

"Right, after you brought it up at me last time. I feel weird about the police report." I explained what I found and I conveyed all what I saw at that time. Not a very pleasant memory but I want to know who did it and why. For about thirty minutes we discussed though.

dr. Ernest was confused why John already knew about the case that happened twenty years ago. John accepted my long term case and I think he would be interested in tracking it down with some additional data from me. Someone knocked on the door.

"Mr. West."

"I'm busy, wait in queue," he snapped at someone who came. I see him as a client for John.

"Wouldn't it be better if we postpone my business for a while, we still have plenty of time to discuss this." John, who was disappointed, had his fun interrupted by the job I had just offered. Nor can I promise that his next client will give him such encouragement. I said goodbye to John and dr. Ernest then invited the guest in and served tea, but John stopped me.

"Why don't you join us?"

"Excuse me?"

"Join us this time."

"I don't mind, even I'm not working today."

"Then make yourself comfortable."

"Okay." I went to a fireplace near my previous seat and picked up a box filled with packs of cigarettes.

"I believe it is yours." I showed it to John.

"How did you find it?"

"The dust on the box is a little thick and had fingermarks that had opened it recently."

"Congratulations, you passed the test."

"I've always wondered why dr. Ernest has been paying close attention to this box while we were talking." i threw the cigarette box at John and dr. Ernest scratched his head because what he did was known to me.

I sat on the chair right in front of dr. Ernest. The client is still confused about what we are doing while he is not around. Dr. Ernest invited him to sit down and tell him what he was going through.

"My name is Adrian Rowland. The reason I came to this place is to ask you to help me reveal what killed my father."

"What happened?"

"He was a scientist for pioneering weapons to win wars in eastern countries."

"So, your father was Dr. Hugo Rowland?" I said interrupting their conversation.

"Yes, sorry, you are...?"

"A concern citizen," John cut in quickly and I said yes.

"Okay, you're right. Hugo Rowland was my father. As a pioneer in the creation of innovative weapons to prevent war between nations he has always dedicated his life to work.

"I'm not interested in that. Let's skip to the point when your father disappeared." Adrian was speechless hearing his consultant's apathy. He was still gathering the words in that dark memory of his.

"That night, while having a family dinner, we were visited by strangers. They are wearing thief mask."

"How did you survive?" Ernest asked.

"As a scientist, my father is also an architect and creates hidden spaces that adults cannot reach. I was just a kid twenty years ago," said Adrian as he took a sip of tea.

"And you managed to survive the ambush."

"Yes, Sir. I saw what happened."

"Can you tell us what happened?"

"They arrested my father and mother. Trying to force him to tell me where the thing they're looking for."

"Did they find it?"

"They stabbed my mother and took my father away. Luckily they had to leave in a hurry because it wasn't long before the Bratginian force arrived and rescued my mother."

"What happened then?"

"We moved to Dofield under an allias and continued our new life with the occasional me trying to find my dad."

"Did you get any new leads?"

"Kind of, but my mother didn't agree that if I approached the case then the people who kidnapped my father will still be hunting us."

"Wise decision," said dr. Ernest filled out his notes.

"But, Adrian, what you are telling us is a story from twenty years ago. You get information from anywhere to go after them. Then why come to us?"

"Because of something happened last night." Me and John said it in sync and made dr. Ernest was amazed even more by Adrian.

"How did you two know that I ran into something last night?"

"Please don't take away my best parts, okay?" John tried to win his fun time.

"John."

"This is your job John, you're the boss." I let him.

"John, stop showing off."

"I am showing off and that is what do." Dr. Ernest sighed because that explanation would only make John feel better by showing off his intellectual prowess. John took an interesting pose to let him deliver his conclusions to his client.

"I saw a piece of paper in your jacket pocket and the small printed form and barcode means you used a plane to get to this city. Also you can see mud spots on your shoes and socks which is unusual for airports which means you departed from Irepool whose airport was still undergoing renovation work in the last two months. You take breakfast at the airport, but you are disappointed with the restaurant and a woman who is interested in you as well as you can be seen from the number written on your handkerchief. Judging from the position of the writing it looks like you two are sitting opposite each other. However, you accidentally spilled your coffee and wiped it with your handkerchief which accidentally removed the number. Seeing that number has faded and you leave it like that because you are no longer interested in it. It's 10:23 am, first flight Irepool at 7:20 am due to refurbishment of renovation team and you flew here for two hours, that means you took a short break maybe smoked then headed here. Another reason is because I smell the familiar smell of tobacco from your forefinger which has just turned yellow after holding it, but you dropped it. That is one of the signs you are anxious and desperate which indicates that something happened last night, am I wrong?" Adrian seemed to take a deep breath as he listened to John's non-stop explanations describing what happened to him.

"You're right... You're absolutely right, bloody hell, I heard you're good, but when I look up close, it's even better."

"That's my job. Ruchester Forces, is there anything you'd like to add?"

"I think you've said everything."

"Don't bore me Grant, come on!"

"Okay." I steadied my seat to see it. I know that I can't be as good as John, but I'm trying to show what I can get from Adrian again.

"I assume you as an athlete, maybe from your college days, what you are still proud of behind your jacket is a shirt with your campus logo on it. I couldn't possibly recognize it as the top school in Dofield. From the way you sit you have an abdominal injury to your leg, so I'm assuming that you are an athlete in a strenuous sport that uses your legs like football or rugby. However, you are a smoker and experienced trauma as a child, so you don't have a problem leaving your prime as an athlete and turning to becoming an insurance officer, which I believe is the main support in your foot health therapy. You gain success, but because of the bad memories that haunt you make you drown in alcohol. I see it clearly from your shaking hand holding your cup. You have a tendency to get drunk when you're nervous and you've been doing that for the last few months. You're trying to hold back your cravings for alcohol because you're going to have a flight this morning, but your body is having a hard time holding it in because your addiction has backfired on you to walk. Of course I knew when you were walking through that door and you bumped your shoulder without knowing it."

"Very brilliant, two genius people in one room showing off their abilities one after another," complained dr. Ernest to us.

"Don't worry about it, Doctor."

"So, Adrian, after twenty years you've been trying to find the truth behind what happened and wasn't it fear or your childhood memories that made you try to find out who did it?"

"Yes, right. Will you help with my case?" John stood up and buttoned his jacket as if getting ready to leave.

"You go first, Adrian. We will follow you."

"And we'll see how far your investigation goes."

"Oh, that matter will be handled by my assistant. I will search from the other side."

"What?" Dr. Ernest was confused after he was tapped on the shoulder by John.

"I just need someone else to track down your investigation even though Ernest has absolutely no idea what he'll be looking for."

"What are you saying? Where are you going?"

"I will find the weapon that all the crowds have lost and been looking for."

"Yes, right. It's the only way to free Adrian from his pursuers."

"I'm going to have a long talk about that John, you better be prepared," annoyed dr. Ernest closed his notepad.

"Do you want to come?"

"I'm free today, but not tomorrow."

"Find excuses not to come work tomorrow, this is more fun, isn't it?" John was happy while wearing his long black coat.

John decided to go somewhere with me while dr. Ernest will travel with Adrian on an investigation. They go after dr. Ernest packed their things. We also left after John hails a taxi.

"Bratginia train station, please."

"Why do we only use the train? I'm sure Adrian paid you for the plane."

"Are you afraid to ride the train?"

"I almost exploded on a train once, especially on the way to Iriepool."

"Good work."

"I am not kidding."

"No, I mean, you were so good at tricking your enemies by making yourself die that they didn't look for you anymore until now."

"Thank You."

"Is there anything else you want to ask?"

"Why am I here?" John smiled at my question.

"I can only follow my instincts that you don't want to leave this matter either."

"What if this ends badly?"

"Like what? Become an enemy to the country for possessing dangerous weapons?"

"Yeah, like that for example."

"You are the family of an important person in this country, and so am I. What else are you afraid of?"

"That is the simplest thing to say like that."

"There is always a way out."

"I hope I don't have to breach my way out." We arrived at Bratginia train station and John received a call from dr. Ernest about his departure for Iriepool and he immediately turned it off. He said that John always told dr. Ernest not to contact him about things that are not important. I'm still confused about how the magical consultant detective communicated with his assistant. Even though I think it's normal for friends who are going to leave to inform first, what I observe from John is a 'workaholic'. He will sniff your case through, nothing more than that. The efforts he made were only a matter of work. Even in this meeting with him, I never heard from him or anyone else talking to him about personal or trivial matters. It feels different to work with famous people compared to workers in general. Not really, I barely saw him exposed by reporters though. He works not as known by others. Nearly every news item covering him does not show his face or accept interviews from him. He only works to satisfy his curiosity and unravel every mystery in every corner of the earth.

"Are you done?"

"What?"

"You are thinking, it seems about me."

"I'm just guessing where you're taking me."

"Just relax."

"Don't mind if I do."

"Good."

Throughout the trip we just busy each other. John, who continues to struggle with his cell phone, I don't really care. To my surprise I also had to be busy with my phone after receiving the call from Tess.

"Hi Grant."

"Hey, Tess, what's up?"

"I just came from your apartment, where are you now?"

"I'm on my way to Irepool. Did I forget something?"

"Too bad, I wanted to invite you to lunch by surprising you. I was surprised that you were gone."

"I'm sorry," a sighing voice from the other person made me feel guilty for her."

"What if we take a raincheck? Surely if you're not busy?"

"I just want to be with you today. Is it that hard for me to make an appointment?"

"I apologize. I also don't plan to meet my friend today. I wish I knew you were coming."

"Who is the friend with you? I hope it's not a woman."

"Of course not. Remember when i was hospitalized with? I am with the private detective I told you about."

"Oh, I didn't know you needed to consult a detective."

"Sorry, personal matter. I can't tell you."

"Grant, you can come up with better reasons than just personal matters."

"I'm sorry..." It didn't feel like my last words had reached Tess and she hung up on the phone. I attempted to send her a lengthy apology message to make up for my mistake.

"You better not do that."

"And now you want to be cupid, John?"

"Take the advice of a consulting detective, I'll consider your case free of charge."

"Is it? Even though you love your job, what do you know about the relationship between men and women?"

"I had... one person..."

"Better rather than nothing."

"And she's gone," his words made me feel guilty for the second time today. I don't feel comfortable continuing this conversation.

"Sorry about that."

"It doesn't matter. She's trying to run away from the trouble she created even though I asked her to join the witness protection program. In the end she died when she got caught and beheaded."

"Did she run from fugitives?"

"No, she was the fugitive."

"Sounds really complicated."

"She tried to threaten some of the country's royal family by possessing their compromising photos and she lives by possessing those secrets."

"And you're the one who caught her."

"She was full of mystery and also a liar."

"You caught her in the end and asked her to join the witness protection program, what a romantic relationship between justice enforcers and criminals."

"A lover's relationship is not only because you enforce justice and she is a criminal, it could be that you are on the same path in your own way."

"Now I understand how consulting detective romance is. Very good advice."

"And your lover is in a state not well to accept the acceptance of your apology."

"Wow... Consulting detective and eavesdropping. You are really a double threat." John just smiled listening to me while playing his cell phone again. This long journey was accompanied only by John. I'm having a hard time doing something where he won't know what I'm going to do.

This day trip didn't feel too rough, but it was boring because it felt like my movements were always being watched by John. He always knows when to interrupt my activities which he can tell from my movements. We take a taxi and arrived at a small inn called Zucci. The name is too flashy even for me or it is true that this place was so crowded that I isn't sure that we would get a room. John asked me to book a lodging room while he would wander around wondering. I just silently complied with his request and met a receptionist behind whom a chef was pacing behind him.

"Good afternoon."

"Good afternoon sir, how can we help you?"

"Two rooms for two, please."

"Of course sir, luckily you didn't miss out on the tour."

"Excuse me, what tour?"

""Oh, I'm sorry sir, I thought you were here because you wanted to tour around what tourists are looking for."

"Ah...south of Iriepool is a hot spring resort."

"That's right, sir. You find out pretty quickly for someone who's here for the first time."

"I just happened to be here even though this is one of the tourist destinations on my list."

"Are you at work or on vacation?"

"I'm not really sure, just following a friend's suggestion to visit this place."

"Okay, enjoy your stay," said the receptionist, handing me two room keys.

"Thank you, but I still want to know about that sightseeing spot."

"That hot spring place used to be a weapons testing ground."

"What happened?"

"It's just a rumour, but if you want to know that in that place used to be a secret lab that was experimenting with making the latest weapons of war."

"What changed?"

"The soldiers who were interviewed at the time said they had a technical error so they blew up the place."

"It's impossible to make a tourist spot, right?"

"After they cleaned up the place. Luckily it wasn't a radiation contaminated area. A hot spring appeared which became the center of attention of the people who wanted to visit it."

"Thank God for the blessing, right?"

"That's what we're always grateful for, isn't it, Billy?" he said to a chef who had started not busy working happened to pass from behind him.

"Such a busy year to manage this place just the two of us."

"Sshh... don't say that!"

"Okay, thanks for the information, gentlemen."

I find John wandering around the outdoor dining area.

"Here you are." I gave him the key room.

"Okay we can rest later, come with me!" John immediately rose from his seat before I sat down. I follow him to an off road car.

"Did you just rent it?"

"Come on up."

"Will you care answer my question?" Without getting anything back from John, I just got in the car and followed wherever he drove.

"So, where are we going?"

"Have you heard of Aloysius II's facility?"

"The secret base that was built after the disaster, right?"

"You can see it now, don't make any sudden moves!"

"What?!" I held back my high voice for John so that the fully armed security forces who were ready to wait for us gave his hand signals for us to stop.

"ID?" said flatly a soldier who asked for John's identity card and John gave it without any hesitation. I'm sure it wasn't his because there was no way the soldier would let him pass as a private investigator.

"You have an ID on Aloysius, how do you do that?"

"Technically it's not mine. It belongs to my brother. I um... stole from him before just in case something like this came up."

"That's great, we will be caught."

"No... not yet."

"Caught after five minutes."

"Maybe longer than that."

"'Welcome to Aloysius, we make dangerous weapons here. You want to have a look? Please come in, we have prepared snacks for you while your friends chat,'" I sarcastically demonstrated someone who was in the facility to greet John. The soldier swiped the identity card John gave him to verify his data. Behold the confirmed identity name as ultra priority. After making sure that the identity approved the personnel who would enter, the soldier returned his identity card to John.

"Through this gate and turn right, sir..."

"Carlson West literally a name that can certainly open every door in this country."

"He has the best grades and position in this government so he was recruited as an agent from my father."

"Don't remind me of the story." We drove toward a place where John could park his car. We got out of the vehicle and walked towards the main door to be greeted by a soldier wearing a beret on his head.

"Sir!! Sir!!" the man's words were ignored by John who tried to speed things up before being caught by someone else.

"Are we in trouble, sir?"

"'Are we in trouble?', sir," said John who felt his presence was disturbing the administrators of the secret facility.

"My name is Corporal Dave Lennon. Your identity indicates that you are personnel with ultra priority, thus, are we in trouble sir?"

"Well, I hope not Corporal, I hope not."

"But we never expected an inspection to take place here."

"Ever heard of the spot check?" I said interrupting the corporal and he wondered who I was and I took out my identity.

"I'm a officer from Ruchester finest. I'm sure you heard about me from Captain Jarrett Briggs, right? and I was asked to accompany this gentleman around this place." I flashed my badge as an active duty constable bearing the name Captain Briggs so he quickly saluted me and I returned the salute.

"Major Louis will not be pleased with this, gentlemen. He wants to meet all of you as immediately."

"We don't have time for that, we need a full tour of this place right now." I said but Lennon seems in doubt, I need a little more push.

"That is an order, Corporal."

"Yes sir!" said Lennon who was alert to my orders and he swiped his identity card then followed by John as a guest.

I noticed that the security system at this facility was extraordinary. People with identification alone may not be able to enter this place without double confirmation from security and personnel inside the facility. These two security systems ensure that everyone who enters has their identity confirmed. Steel doors opened slowly inside the facility. John measured the time since he swiped his ID. It seemed the fake data would arrive in the time John had estimated. We headed for the elevator and again Lennon and John swiped their cards. This makes me very depressed want to run away from here. Lennon pressed the B5 button from the farthest elevator down, which was B10.

"How deep does this lift go down?"

"Deep enough, sir."

"Are there any suspicious people coming in and out of here with experimental items?"

"He must have a help from security, sir. Major Louis is very strict with this weapon facility espionage."

"So what's on the B10 floor?"

"That is where we dispose of the remains of unused materials, sir." The elevator doors opened and I was dazzled by this bright light. After I got used to the retina of my eyes to the light with which they work. We walked following Corporal Lennon.

"So what are you guys doing here?"

"Yes, Sir? I thought you already knew." I spontaneously dumbfounded.

"Because you came here for an inspection."

"I'm not an expert, am I?"

"During the war twenty years ago, a scientist succeeded in creating a dangerous chemical weapon whose power was capable of scorching a country to the ground. Too bad at that time there was not enough protocol to protect him from being kidnapped by the enemy. Therefore, many scientists here are trying to replicate their work from obsolete records," explained Lennon showing us the activities of the researchers in their hazard suits testing liquids whose shape I am not very familiar with. Even though I myself am a forensic researcher who examines chemical elements as well.

"Any ideas on what the scientist created?"

"We still don't understand it for sure. A common indication of the scientific record is some kind of mercury (mercury/silver water)," Lennon continued his way through the midst of a laboratory full of researchers. I tried to whisper a discussion with John without Lennon noticing.

"There's no way it's mercury."

"I know, no human can control mercury to make a bomb."

"The components are too heavy, unless there is a magnet that can move it at will, it's still a mystery how it was made into a bomb."

"So do they."

"Who's this?" said a middle-aged man with his signature laugh.

"Dr. Luke, they are the ultra priority for inspections."

"Really? It's great to see new faces." Me and John just gave a smile.

"What is your role here dr. Luke?"

"Am I allowed to speak here?"

"Maybe you should talk, Doctor."

"I'm afraid I can't, this is a secret facility, right?"

"We just wanted to ask how far your role in Aloysius is?" I said to mediate his suspicions.

"I'm just supervising the security of this job. You all know that combining two chemicals can be dangerous if not closely monitored. We don't want what happened before to happen again."

"Were you also there when the facility exploded?"

"Yeah, it just so happened that I was outside and I survived the evacuation which lasted less than five minutes."

"Is that so? I think we're done here Corporal."

"Wait, that's it?"

"Yes, That will be all. This way, right?" John turned around from where we were and we seemed to have to go back considering the time we had spent here was already twenty minutes from what had been prepared. Things took a turn for the worse when we found out that John wasn't the man on the ID.

An operator answered the phone by asking several things to the person he was talking to. The system goes from one person to another to verify information from data that seems hard to believe from data administrators. Until finally the information reached a secretary who then she immediately called her boss. A cellphone lights up in the middle of the silence room which is being enjoyed by someone wearing a white suit. That's right, none other than Phill calmly reading a newspaper. He was surprised by the contents of the message he received from his secretary in the form of a 'joke' that was carried out by his younger brother in a secret facility of Aloysius II. He types a message and sends it in the middle of a headache seeing his brother's behavior. A message arrives on John's cell phone. He laughed sarcastically reading the contents of the message from his brother.

"It's been twenty-two minutes, my brother is getting slower."

John stepped quickly and first and swiped his card. Lennon offset his guest who wanted to hurry without the slightest suspicion he swiped his card until the elevator door opened. Without us thinking that dr. Luke also followed us.

"Excuse me, gentlemen, if you don't mind," of course we said nothing until the elevator doors closed and left the basement floor to the ground floor. However, unfortunately the unexpected happened. Someone was waiting for us in front of the elevator whose figure was immediately visible. He was waiting for us to come via the elevator as the only way out. He is Mayor Louis as the supreme owner of this facility.

"This is really outrageous! Why wasn't I informed?" I'm sure Lennon would be in trouble if he reported his superiors. Therefore I think it's time I try to be nice with him here.

"Major Louis, it is a pleasure to see you here. We are satisfied with the safety of this place, aren't we, Mr. West?" I offered my hand to shake, but Major Louis did not take my hand in response. John just ignored him through behind me and passed him. I followed John and tried not to get involved in this matter any further.

"What's going on here?"

"Aloysius II is a secret place so eliminate this kind of bureaucracy, an inspection!"

"We're just implementing a new policy because this place can't be unmonitored for too long... keep going!" whispered John to tell me to keep going.

"Sir!" Corporal Lennon sounded the alarm and began protocol shutting the premises down. The sound of the alarm sirens in this facility is like an alarm ringing loudly in my head.

"Your ID is no longer valid."

"What? Why?"

"There seems to be something wrong here, Major."

"Of course you do, who are you exactly?" the worst times I expected had come. Major Louis saw for himself the ID card given to him by John and Major Louis quickly recognized the mistake.

"Of course he's not Carlson West, who are you?"

"It's just a computer error, Major, it will be noted in the report, right?"

"What are you guys doing here..."

"It's okay Major I know who these gentlemen are."

"Do you?"

"I'm a little slow to recognize someone's face and Mr. West is someone I didn't expect to meet here."

"Well..." this bad incident escalated to the danger that someone would recognize John's face. We absolutely cannot stop this person from saying the name.

"Nice to see you here, Carlson."

"Is it?" John took his identity card which was handed back by Major Louis.

"I am honored to hear you speak at the peace conference of nations in... Albama, am I not?

"A middle eastern country, Kashir."

"Kashir, yes, absolutely right. Major, this is really Mr. Carlson West. There must be an mistake." Major Louis gave Corporal Lennon the head signal to turn off the alarm and he quickly did so. The situation had calmed down somewhat thanks to the help from someone I didn't expect.

"On your head be it, dr. Luke." The scientist chuckled at him and asked Major Louis to let him take his guests out. We, who remained silent until we left the facility, were almost given the death penalty for espionage using the names of important people in this country. I couldn't bear to think about the danger we were in if we were still inside the facility and they could figure out who we were.

"Thank You."

"It's about Adrian, isn't it?"

"Keep going!"

"I know Adiran is in trouble, but who would have thought he went to see a famous consulting detective."

"You know about me?"

"I follow every news about you and also the cases you solve."

"Thank You."

"And who is he? Isn't your assistant dr. Ernest?"

"I just need extra man to accompany me."

"We really thank you for saving us from the danger just now."

"Of course, sir."

"You know about Adrian and his late father?"

"I only know Hugo Rowland, he was my mentor."

"Not a bit with Adrian?"

"He was simply expressing the loss of his father by showing us as the ones responsible for the incident."

"So there's nothing you can tell us?"

"Well, Mr West, I wanted to tell you, but..." Dr. Luke looked around and he saw Major Louis still watching our movements.

"It's not safe to talk in here, I'll give you my cell number and we can talk outside."

"Thank you, again and for this."

"Anytime, gentlemen," we turned around and dr. Luke also left us back to his place of work.

"That was very close."

"So, this facility makes a replication of the late Hugo Rowland's creation as the best chemical weapons pioneer in this country."

"We have to get ahead of them by finding out what he created back then."

"Looks like we can gather at Adrian's place today."

"We have got our share, the rest will be found by Dr. Ernest."

"Let's go!" we boarded the car and left the heavily guarded base. We drive to Adrian's house which is quite far from here.

We drive for more than two hours until we arrive at a large house, but it looked like the yard had not been taken care of. Lots of long grass also spreading branches from trees that hit the walls of the house. John hurriedly knocked on the door, Adrian opened it and ushered us in.

"Dr. Ernest was already waiting in my library room. Please, gentlemen." We entered the library and found dr. Ernest is reading books.

"Hey," said Dr. Ernest, who is under pressure, reads all the material Adrian has prepared regarding his father's research.

"Did you get anything?"

"I don't really understand chemistry."

"Of course you are."

"Why did you put me in a task like this?"

"I need a person of average mind to search for clues with luck."

"You're out of luck with that. I don't understand chemistry for weaponry at all."

"That's not far from my expectations, Doctor."

"Here it is, your annoying attitude is putting me in the wrong place."

"Where are you going?"

"I just want to make coffee," said dr. Ernest from behind the room left us. We noticed that the amount of material Adrian had prepared was enormous. I recognize him for making all of this besides living his miserable life. Many people vent their frustration or curiosity by doing something very unusual and produce this kind of result, but this is too much for even the most skilled. I don't know how much it cost to get a result like this.

Excuse me, Adrian.

"What's wrong, Mr. Dylan?" it seems that Adrian knows me from dr. Ernest had told him about it when he was here.

"Did your late father leave all of this to you?"

"Yes, that is true."

"Ah, sorry for asking. Excuse me for a moment." I picked up my ringing cell phone. I seem to have forgotten that today I am skipping work.

"Grant, why didn't you come in today?"

"I'm sorry, Eddie. Looks like I can't go to work today. Am I feeling unwell."

"Is it true? Tess visits you, but you say you won't be there for a few days. Does this have anything to do with your illness?"

"That...."

"I know, son. You're on a case, right?"

"How do you know?"

"I've been working for almost two decades and I know how people try to lie to detectives like me."

"I'm so sorry about that."

"Fine, I'll tell to Captain, just hurry home. You're going to make things difficult for Caith."

"I think I remember something. Thanks for the help, Inspector." I hung up and tried to reach Caith.

"Hey Caith. Are you there?"

"Oh, Hi, Grant. Did I forget something?"

"No, I want to apologize if I can't come to work today," I explained to Caith and it seemed like she didn't hear me and was talking to someone there.

"I'm back. The inspector just told me about you being not well."

"I just said that."

"Don't worry about work, take a rest."

"I'm sorry and thank you." I conclude and I go back into the room with Dr. Ernest bringing coffee for him and for John. He was sorry he couldn't take more than two and Adrian was making them for him and for me. I'm fine with that. I tried to start their work by tracing the results of an investigation by Adrian who was still puzzled about what his father was making.

In a different place with the same time, the sound of footsteps running hastily in a large office. A man who was running glanced at his watch and he accelerated his run. He headed for a door that read 'Director' on the front door and he opened it without knocking first. The two people in the room were surprised during their conversation that someone had entered without knocking first as if emergency information had come to him.

"What is it?"

"Sir, we have a marker from intel. They mentioned that this information is Priority One Alpha." Mr. Director just put down his pen while looking down on what information his intelligence provided.

"Something they call 'Nightshade'."

"Shut up!" The man was shocked to hear the director suddenly snap at him after hearing a word that he felt was taboo for others to hear. The director asked everyone to leave the room. After the door closed and no one would hear him anymore, he made a call from his office phone.

"Find Jessica Rachel for me!"

A footstep walked down the hall of a hotel. He was none other than the director who had been told where the whereabouts of the woman he was looking for. In front of room number 3033 the director knocked on the door and in a few moments the door opened slightly and only a woman's face appeared with a flustered expression.

"Director Sean? I'm with someone right now." The director forced his way into the room and saw the bodies of three dead men on the floor.

"Still busy it seems."

"What can I say, I'm just bored."

"Whatever you are doing here, I want your focus to another mission." The director handed the file to the woman and she opened it.

"Your old friend seems to want to try to get ahead of us."

"Are you sure about this information, Director?"

"You doubt you can do it because he's your friend?" said the man doubting the woman named Jessica.

"It's time to choose the side, Jessica," the man threatened so that the woman just looked down and didn't face the person who was ordering her.

Back in a library with four other people trying to get their hands on what everyone has been chasing in the last twenty years. Me, John, and dr. Ernest is accompanied by Adrian Rowland who is still busy discussing chasing the missing dangerous object.

"In a way I'm relieved the weapon is nowhere to be found, isn't that a win for everyone?"

"Temporarily put your naïve thoughts aside, Doctor."

"Has it ever occurred to you that if you had that weapon in your hand, what would you do?"

"Disarm it, give it to the Ruchester unit and it will be in safe hands."

"Safe? No offense, Grant, other nations knowing that a weapon is in our country's hands indicates that our nation will have weapon to start a war."

"That's so stupid. Why should our country start a war?"

"Let the stupid me explain to you. Assume each country's war power on a scale. Right now they are all about equal. Then, you put in this latest and greatest weapon and the balance will be broken and they want to gain the upper hand by taking that weapon."

"Your point?"

"Open your eyes genius, our lives are in danger too if we look for that weapon." John's cell phone rang and he only glanced a little from the notification.

"Looks like you've had bad luck, Doctor," he said holding the cellphone to his ear.

"What?"

"It seems that I was asked by my superiors to arrest you." A woman's voice is on the other side of John's cell phone.

"I'm glad you haven't done that by now."

"Don't feel happy just yet, I have to do it or they will kill me."

"Do what you have to do." John hung up on her and I sensed that we were being targeted by mercenaries, which surprised him why did he tell John first before coming to him? I, who like a new kid joined the association of consulting doctors and detectives, felt more and more interested in what they could give me.

"Who called you?"

"Jesie."

"Oh, God, looks like she's still alive."

"Who is Jessie?" I asked curiously.

"Not one word from you, Doctor."

"His girlfriend."

"I seem confused." I tried to level their conversation.

"Not one word from you, Ruchester finest."

"Okay, I won't ask."

"Lucky for us Jesie gave us a warning before she came to us."

"From what we already know, right?"

"We can assume we're in danger from the other assassins."

"However, we still haven't been able to get any signs of what the object looked like and where it was hidden by Adrian's father."

"So, what do we do now?"

"Is there someone directly involved with your father? It would be great if he is still alive."

"An ex-marine, dr. Curtis, he's here. He is also a psychologist."

"Very good, where can we find him?"

"It's getting dark, I think he's having a meeting right now."

"Meeting?"

"Yeah, sort of a group meeting of ex army talking about their past."

"How bad his past?"

"He's a Marine who retired because he injured his leg after hitting an IED (Improvised Explosive Device)."

"That means we're looking for a cripple," John gave a sarcasm.

"No, Mr. West, he has a prosthetic leg on his left."

"Good to know, looks like my Doctor and Grant will be seeing him."

"You're not coming?"

"I have no business with people without legs."

"He was a soldier, John, they fought until they were no longer of use when they were injured and the country left them."

"Not really."

"Let's go, Grant!"

"Lead the way, Doctor." Dr. Ernest and I entered a building with a welcome written on the door. There is no one we meet when we enter the door and there are voices talking through the dark passage and light shining through the door. I draw closer to the sound followed by dr. Ernest. The voice that is increasingly heard is an outpouring of someone's bad experience. I watch over the situation from behind the door to make sure my presence don't disturb them. A large, well-dressed man with a blue tie signaled me to enter the room without disturbing the person who was talking. I notice that there were two empty chairs close together and I feel sure that we should sit in those places and join them.

The sad story after story that they felt opened my eyes on how a soldier who had been discharged was treated. I remembered that dr. Ernest himself was a doctor who was dismissed from duty because he got a gunshot wound. He earned his medical degree before joining the country's military service. It's strange to hear that people who play the role of saving human lives actually take other people's lives. My daydream ends there. I think dr. Ernest is also suitable to gather here because I feel that everyone here has more or less the same history.

"The president gave this medal to me. When I come home, what do I get? They just spit at me."

"Did you serve the country at that time? Or expect thanks?" those words made the person who was showing off the president's medal speechless.

"We all serve, none of them expect that. You're lucky to be able to flaunt your medal everywhere, not lose limbs," said the person while tapping his leg which I'm sure is the prosthetic leg he's using. Now I know that the man who brought us in was Dr. Curtis himself.

"Look at all of you, just losers sitting around like this, whining about being abandoned by the country."

"Watch your tongue, Moslow!"

"The bottom line is that we have the same problems and therefore we must stick together to support each other. No one recognizes any of our problems other than ourselves."

"Whatever!" muttered the man named Moslow as he mocked them.

"Those words of yours will catch you one day, Moslow."

"Okay, I'm out of here!" he said annoyed and left the room with his shout insulting the people gathered.

"All right everyone, same time next week, OK?"

"Thank you, Curtis," echoed the crowd. They greeted each other until they reached us. The participants left the place while throwing away their drinking glass trash near the exit. The remaining dr. Curtis was the one who was still busy tidying up the chairs used by the members and he folded them and then tidied them in place.

"Let me guess, you guys came here to ask me right?"

"No, um... may I know your name, sir?"

"Hoyd Curtis, former marine, and you are?"

"Harry Ernest, former captain of batalion 8."

"Eagle Team? An honor to meet you?"

"Please, we are both retired, it's all in the past."

"How can I help you, gentlemen?"

"Forgive us if we want to ask about the bad memories, Mr Curtis."

"How far from my past do you want to ask?"

"It's about Hugo Rowland."

"Ah, are you guys going to kill me after I tell you everything?"

"Is everyone trying to kill you knowing all that?" I asked curious about what dr. Curtis with this information he has.

"Okay, I believe you guys aren't after my life. So, I'll tell you guys."

Curtis left three stools that he still hadn't made and asked us to sit down to hear his story. He also did not forget to serve coffee that he had made from the pantry table which provided coffee or tea that could be taken by visitors who came to join him when holding meetings. Curtis still had the coffee he had left before. This freshly brewed coffee is still very hot. Psychologically, what I read is that if a psychologist wants to talk and serve hot drinks like coffee or tea, it indicates that this story takes a long time or he wants to assess how we behave when we receive hot drinks, whether we rush to drink it or enjoy what the drink giver has to offer. Of course my mind was signaling that it was as if we were being tested by Curtis or was it just my feeling seeing dr. Ernest enjoyed this hot drink casually and he enjoyed it.

"Thanks for the coffee, Doctor."

"So you know about me?"

"Just a general matter regarding how long you served and the characteristics given by others namely your prosthetic leg."

"-slurping coffee, hmm... sorry, can I have some sugar please?" I asked spontaneously as if interrupting their conversation. I looked at the face of dr. Ernest was as annoyed as he was at John. I was silent for a few moments until Curtis pointed out the table where he was making coffee to get some sugar. Of course I took no more than a cube and I returned to their conversation.

"This is what I got after trying to block the breakthrough of the guerrilla army. I tried to bandage my own leg so it wouldn't bleed out. Then I went home and got sponsored by my friends to build this group."

"Back to our original purpose, is it true that you were assigned to be the bodyguard of a scientist named Hugo Rowland?"

"Yes, a year before I received an injury to my leg. You can see in my hair where there are stitches."

"What happened?"

"The mercenaries are after him. They are really professional. I'm lucky their bullet just grazed my head and I lost consciousness from loss of blood. They ignored those of us who were on duty and hastily kidnapped Professor Hugo."

"How did you get the information if the kidnapper was in a hurry?" I asked in amazement at the thought of him losing consciousness but knowing full well the kidnapper didn't have long to carry out his action.

"Of course I was interrogated by headquarters why I'm still alive. A relief team has come because they informed us of the mercenaries arrival."

"So help arrived so late that Professor Hugo was nowhere to be found when they arrived."

"That's right, my superiors confirmed it through the surveillance cameras that weren't tampered with by the kidnappers."

"Okay, we're not asking about how she was actually kidnapped. We want to know what he created. Do you have any knowledge of that?"

"So you're looking for that weapon?"

"As far as we're concerned, yes."

"What do you want with that weapon?"

"We just want that weapon gone from earth."

"I'm glad to hear that as much as I believe you guys."

"Thank you, Doctor Curtis."

"Once when I brought an aluminum box with a size of 50x50 with 80cm high. I think it weighs about 20kg. After delivering the item and checking the contents, I was asked to take a look."

"What do you see?"

"A bomb with a timer attached which led me to believe it was a bomb was the component in the tube that glowed brightly."

"Can you describe those components?"

"Glowing red, looks like liquid, but I'm not sure either."

"Oh Lord."

"What's wrong, Grant?"

"It's red mercury."

"Oh… damn it!" dr. Ernest let out a deep breath hearing the object of his disaster I mentioned.

"What are we talking about, sir?"

"In 195X, when the cold war was going on, many countries were competing to make the strongest weapon. Many say that the trial of making weapons culminated with the appearance of this red mercury."

"I heard that this red mercury substance itself never existed."

"Of course it was hidden to prevent its re-creation."

"And now that weapon is being coveted by everyone."

"We need more than hope that these weapons are not misused by people who want to start another war."

"I totally agree with that."

"Thank you for your time, Doctor Curtis."

"Good luck with your mission Sir and Doctor."

"Keep yourself safe," dr. Ernest greeted him and we left Curtis. Dr. Ernest immediately called John to tell him what we had.

"John, we already know what kind of substance was in the weapon."

"Let me guess, the legendary substance called red mercury, right?"

"How do you know? You didn't come here at all."

"I'm just using the process of elimination."

"It's good that you know about it. It seems that the weapon is indeed targeted because they want to use it to trigger the next war."

"Whoever has the strongest hand is able to make a new war to win it."

"Any ideas where we should look for it?"

"Pack your things, we'll be leaving tomorrow morning."

We continued our journey by plane to arrive in the northern country of Great Buturea. Our journey lasted long enough to finally land. I thought I could go sightseeing in this town, but John took us in his rented Jeep to

45

explore the mountains. he asked dr. Ernest to navigate the journey until we arrived at a bridge. Our car was suddenly stopped by John just about to cross the bridge.

"Why are we stopping?" ask dr. Ernest and saw John's face just silently staring ahead. Me and dr. Ernest followed his gaze and saw that there was a person standing at the end of the bridge in the direction we were going with a sniper in hand. He was wearing a knitted woolen cap, a typical cold weather army dress and enough boots to convince me that the person standing on the other side was Jesie, the person John loved.

"How did she know we were coming?"

"Must be from his superiors." Jesie just stared at us silently, not looking like a friend nor looking like an enemy. His silence raises a question mark whether he's really chasing us just to finish us off or he's setting a trap by catching us here."

"Why didn't she shoot us?"

"I don't know yet, everyone don't move from your seats." John surveyed the situation and saw out his car window a sign of the wind blowing behind us. John backed up the car slowly and Jesie prepared to fire her gun at us.

Bang!

A jeep caught fire in the grass on the right side of the bridge. Jesie just looked at the car and the three burnt corpses with a blank stare. Dr. Ernest approached Jesie following what Jesie had seen earlier.

"Where exactly do you keep the bodies?"

"In my fridge."

"Jessica," John said softly.

"Oh, John, dear." They hugged each other.

"Don't think anything, Grant," he snapped at me who didn't say anything.

"Just as you like, mother hen."

"Hoo... I like him. Where did you find a good specimen?"

"It's okay, Grant, she always like this," interjected Dr. Ernest while patting my shoulder.

"We have twenty-four hours to move without being noticed by the other side."

"So this is how you fake your death?"

"Relax, I'm not like you who can control the media to prove your death."

"It wasn't my idea."

"Whatever."

We moved off the bridge and headed back to town. Where Jesie showed us a safe house to hide. In this hiding place Jesie shares with us a data that she has.

"You're right, John. I stole intel from them and it looks like nightshade is indeed missing in this town."

"Any idea where it might have stashed?"

"You're not going to like it."

We walked towards the center of Buturea Raya. We walked together with dr. Ernest brought a tool bag that Jesie gave him which he thought was a bit heavy. Our journey was not that far, I who had wanted to look around became dispersed after Jesie stopped our journey and was confronted by a large, towering building and I had only ever seen it on television.

"You must be kidding."

"No, this is what we will face."

"Great Buturea Intelligence Bureau."

"Why is it here?"

"Here is where the last tracking is, but no one is aware of it."

"No one can search in this sacred place."

"So do we, right?"

"Not really."

Jesie led us away from the building to the shopping area. She points out that there is one path that has been closed by the changing times and forgotten by everyone. I'm still wondering where Jesie got this information. This information is absolutely no one knows, but she can get it.

"This is where we will enter."

"Big Belly Burgers?"

"Complete with chicken and chips."

"Are you guys hungry?" I asked, still confused. Jesie asked John to order foods while we followed her to a restroom in the back. Dr. Ernest opened the contents of his bag that he had brought earlier. The contents are a large hammer to dismantle the tiles on the wall, a kind of uniform, a stun gun, and some grenades. John returns with his food and drinks order were enjoyed while waiting for dr. Ernest dismantled the wall. We wait casually even though we were enjoying our food in an unnatural environment while waiting for the demolition of the wall to be completed. I guard the door by giving a sign 'under construction', luckily they have more than one toilet so I don't have to bother asking other people to go look for a toilet which might be far from here. About thirty minutes later, dr. Ernest opened a large gap that adults could enter. He opens one brick that was blocking it using his foot. John shines a flashlight on the secret passage.

"Looks like this passage leads to the bureau."

"Okay, we'll look into it."

"Lock the door! Don't let anyone else see this!" Jesie commanded me.

We walked down a narrow passage that only one person could pass through. Dr. Ernest is the vanguard and I am the last one holding the flashlight. Of course at that time we are nervous that if we walked out of this tunnel we would be met by intelligence agents ready to arrest us. Of course the punishment for infiltrating the intelligence building is life imprisonment or the death penalty. Flashlight dr. Ernest hit a door that is in front of him.

"What do you think is behind that door?"

"Agents?"

"Wait, I have a stun gun." Dr. Ernest came out slowly and he had already confirmed that no one was around the room. It turns out that this is an underground server room that is not guarded by anyone. Instantly we felt relieved after exiting the narrow passage, but the main plan was still going on. Dr. Ernest also took out a general's uniform that he had as well as an elite officer's uniform such as a captain and a uniform for women.

"We need one person to guard here, I have three uniforms for us to wear undercover."

"I think it will be easy for us to determine who is on guard for people who speak their language."

"Who can speak the Buturea Raya accent?" I asked, of course John turned to his partner, dr. Ernest.

"That's very good advice, Grant."

"I'm just saying. No one has rejected my idea since earlier."

"Your advice said I should be here to make sure no one gets into this place."

"That is an important task, doctor! They will lock this place to catch any intruders."

"Okay, I'll do what I can."

"Use the gas leak excuse, it works every time."

We go out in our uniforms letting Jesie lead the way in hers now. She is very famous here, it must be fine for her to be in this place. But on the other hand, we are nobody, it would be strange if civilians wearing normal clothes wander around here even if they were brought by someone who has an important role in the bureau. We walk and follow Jesie who is still confused to find a place where she knew the dangerous object was stored. Arrive in an old wardrobe that is very dusty. Jesie gives the key to John and he uses his strength to open the object that was completely unused. The door opened and we made sure that no one came near us because the noise unlocked the cupboard. I look inside the cupboards there are files and an aluminum box the size dr. Curtis said before. I feel certain that this is the bomb they had been looking for. I take it and open the box in front of John and Jesie. A red light shone as soon as the box was opened and pressed a deep red on our faces. Only with red canisters accompanied by an inactive timer. We try to be inconspicuous after noticing its presence. John carries it carefully while Jesie and I follow him and cover our postures so that no one else would notice the box. We try to walk unhurriedly so as not to arouse suspicion by those who passed us. I admire John's courage to infiltrate this place without any worries. I see dr. Ernest who was getting bored keeping watch there. He tried to stay on his feet.

"What took you so long?"

"Keep your mouth shut and get inside!" We entered the server room again and quickly packed up our things. Without asking too many questions, Dr. Ernest follows us packing and returning to the Big Belly Burger restaurant via a secret passage. Jesie tries to close the secret door using the grenade she has and destroys the secret passage so no one else will know. We try to stay inconspicuous out of the restaurant and back to the safe house.

We made it back to the safe house without any hindrance. John tries to explain what he have found and the items seemed to be real. Dr. Ernest was excited that the mission this time was a success. He carries a bottle of champagne to celebrate the difficulty of this task and felt that he had avoided danger.

"Let's celebrate this success, thank you Jesie for providing champagne in this house," cheered Dr. Ernest pouring champagne into glasses and giving them to me, John and Jesie.

"*Vashe zdorov'ye*!" Jesie cheered inviting us to toast to celebrate this success. We both raised our glasses and enjoyed the celebration. I feel happy for a moment when I saw John who was just glum by drinking a little of his champagne. a bad feeling comes from the look on his face when he received a call from someone. He asks for a moment and steps away from us to pick up his ringing cell phone.

"What is it?"

"Listen to me, dear brother!"

"Hello, brother dear, it's a rare opportunity for you to call me. Usually you would pass it on to me through dr. Ernest, right?"

"Are you alone?"

"Right now, yes."

"Your girlfriend didn't just happen to be there knowing where nightshade was. He was informed by someone from inside."

"What?"

"Get up, stupid brother! It's a setup!" call cut off abruptly.

"John," a low voice from behind John called him so he slowly looked behind him.

"...."

"Your brother called you, right?" Jesie pointed a gun at John from behind.

"Put down your cellphone and walk." John had no choice but to follow Jesie's orders until he got to me and dr. Ernest who was still enjoying his drink. I was just surprised that my guess was right 'Jesie is going to set us up'.

"Boys, don't try to take your weapons."

"Just do what she says." John, who was still being held at gunpoint to walk in front of Jesie, decided not to counterattack Jesie.

"Why? I always knew you'd be a fool if you met her, John."

"Calm down, Doctor."

"I won't calm down this time!"

"Dr. Ernest, you always suspect me but not when John is on my side, right?"

"I like to see you try to finish off all three of us at once."

"I wouldn't bother doing it myself." Enter the footsteps that break into this safe house, soldiers in uniform from Buturea Raya. They immediately took up positions to detain us and threatened to shoot at any sudden movements.

"You work together with them, why am I not surprised?" dr. Ernest's mind was getting tired of his experience of always being played by Jesie for as long as they had known her.

"We don't work with her, but she works with me," said someone who then entered after feeling that this room had been successfully secured.

"So, you are Director Sean," said John who saw who was controlling the operation of all this.

"Don't feel offended, boys! From the beginning Jessica is on our side. I really didn't think he could get it with just a little help from me."

"Why do you want Nightshade?"

"Of course, my country needs a new warhead to overcome the scale that has balanced after decades, what else?"

"Jesie, listen to me, this thing should not be owned by anyone. Not your government, nor mine."

"I'm sorry handsome, nothing personal. I have orders."

"This is not about orders. It's about right or wrong!" Jesie was silent listening to John's words and director Sean was starting to run out of patience to take us and use the weapons of mass destruction in his hands. We are lead away by soldiers and sees Sean turning his back on us.

"Don't worry fellas, you will be deported to your own country. We also have footage of you infiltrating the bureau, if that's what you call genius, right, consulting detective?"

"You will regret it later!" John threatens them and we are taken away from the safe house and we wait to see what we will face in court.

We are in a military utility truck and were taken without being able to see anywhere because our faces were covered with black cloth. Complete with handcuffs, we can't do anything without visual power to support our abilities. The road is not so good we pass based on the shock of the tires on the ground that is not so flat. Sean said he would deport us, I guessed our goal was to go to a military base at countryside of Great Buturea. The journey took a very long time, not only was the weather cold enough to make my body shiver but the handcuffs felt uncomfortable on my wrists. The trucks stop and the soldiers drop us off like criminals who need no pity. They remove my blindfold and my eyes which were still adjusting to the lighting outside took me a while to realize we were at the foot of a mountain. This inland side is fills with army headquarters with barracks, shooting ranges, and vehicle repair shops. My body was pushed by them and taken to walk towards a wooden pole that was staked in a row. I feel like this is the end of my life because it's a execution place. They didn't drop John off, he was still left in the truck.

"I only need a consulting detective, execute the rest!" Sean's orders left us in his luxury car to take John. me and dr. Ernest is being tied up for target shooting by tying our arms up with iron chains. While on the feet only tied using a rope. Somehow I didn't feel the least bit panicked.

"Why are you still calmed, Grant?"

"I don't know, maybe because I've seen this before."

"I swear, if I die, I will haunt them!"

"Pfft... You have a very good imagination, Doctor."

"Don't let me haunt over you too!" On cue the soldiers were getting ready to shoot us. They put six shooters to execute two people. Dr. Ernest getting more panicked made me want to work on him even more.

"If we can get out of this situation, who are you going to beat up first?"

"Of course I'll beat up that psychopath couple!" Dr. Ernest's anger was ignored by the soldiers who kept aiming at us. I of course saw the flash sign from afar. I still don't know who it is and for sure it will save us.

'Bang! 'Bang! A shot from a long range rifle attacked the soldiers and they scattered for cover. The shoot that hit one of the six executors only hit the non-lethal part. I know those who are not busy with us are widening my arms to give the marksman the best aim.

'Bang! The next shot hit my chain and freed my hands from the shackles though the chain still locked on my wrist. I chased the executors and beat up two people who were near me. I was able to take the gun from him and attack him with the ease of hitting the gun in his face. They've all been disabled. It was safe and I took my rifle and walked over to dr. Ernest.

"Close your eyes, Doctor." My shot shattered the chains that held dr. Ernest, then he untied his legs.

"Who's that? Who saved us?"

"You won't like to hear that." me and dr. Ernest ran towards the direction of the gunshots that saved us. Nearly three kilometers away she took up her firing position. When we got closer to her, she is packing her things into a red sports car.

"No way, what's going on here?"

"Look, do you feel better now?" I said, trying to catch my breath after a long run.

"I don't understand what's going on here?"

"Well Doctor, I think this is what John has planned."

"Nice to see you again, Doctor."

"No! She will betray us again. I won't believe her!"

"Doctor, take a deep breath." Dr. Ernest tried to follow my suggestion and he tried to calm down in the midst of his panic.

"How many times have you been betrayed by Jesie?"

"Everything I've ever had?"

"Yes."

"Including today?"

"Yap, how many?"

"Seven times. She tried to betray us seven times... EIGHT TIMES! fucking Dofield!"

"Look at you, doctor."

"What are you trying to talk about."

"Still in one piece, isn't it."

"He continues to dwell on the past, officer."

"I guess so," I joked to all of dr. Ernest became yawning lost because he was too embarrassed.

"Get on, we have to catch John!"

"It's lucky you're not dead, Doctor," I said, still laughing at Dr. Ernest. He was still annoyed in his muttering.

"So, can you explain about your plans with John."

"I didn't expect Director Sean to take action to execute you guys, I'm sorry for that."

"My God, I thought I would die from being shot by them at that time."

"Shut up, Doctor!" I said simultaneously with Jesie.

"For God's Sake, can you two not suddenly being together to push me away?" annoyed dr. Ernest who has no supporters at all

"Where is John now?"

"Great Buturea military base airport."

"What are we dealing with?"

"Dozens of soldiers, not to mention infiltrating a military cargo plane is not easy."

"Doctor, can you drive this Huracan?"

"Don't bother asking, Grant. I can't have a luxury car like Lamborghini."

"Then you should watch Jesie how to use it. Is this a convertible Jesie?"

"Yes of course."

"Leave the infiltrating the cargo plane to me, get us there!"

"I'll show you what this thing can do." Jesie sped as fast as she could toward the center of town. Our execution site is in the opposite direction to the military airport. This considerable distance will take too much time if you use an ordinary car. Jesie correctly brought her V10 engined vehicle and she is driving at 200 km/h. The atmosphere of this deserted city benefits us from speeding to our heart's content by inviting lots of cops trying to stop us. It's not easy for them to chase super sports cars. In less than ten minutes we had left the downtown and headed for the quiet road leading to the military airstrip.

"Hold on John," muttered Jesie obliviously and dr. Ernest focused on Jesie's driving style. I didn't expect it to come out of her mouth or it was just an act, I never know.

"Look! The airport is in sight!" I shouted pointing to the airport ahead with lots of soldiers circling around the cargo plane. I'm still amazed by the size of the cargo plane that says 'G.B. Airforce'. Never mind no need to look at things that detailed. I had to start executing this plan so I could follow John onto the plane.

"We have arrived!"

"Looks like they have started packing," I responded seeing them starting to disperse away from the cargo plane using the binoculars given by Jesie.

"Your turn, Doctor."

"It is time?"

"Do it now or the police who have started their pursuit will catch us back!"

"All right, annoying lady!" Dr. Ernest starts driving the car and speeds towards the military airport.

John is currently the one who finds himself in the custody of four people along with director Sean who is escorting him. John is currently dealing with who is behind all these problems.

"So what about Rowland's son? Is he still alive?"

"…"

"Your presence here confirms that he is still alive."

"Your deductions are excellent even if they are baseless."

"That's called the investigator's instinct, my friend."

"What are you going to do with nightshade?"

"Want to share your imagination?"

"Your desire to destroy a country doesn't interest me in sharing to you."

"Let me humor you," he said as he opened the aluminum box.

"First of all, I will start the timer on this bomb." Sean turned on the timer and the clock was set it seemed from the start with five hours running backwards.

"As you know, the flight from here to the downtown of your country takes four hours and 30 minutes. We will give you ten minutes to escape from this explosion."

"You bastard!"

"Don't worry about it, I'll personally throw it through that cargo door."

"Sir!" said the pilot who shouted for his boss.

"What is it? Don't interrupt me with my guests!"

"Someone broke into the military base."

"What happened?"

"They broke through the fence and at high speed chased us."

"Quickly take this plane off! They will get into the plane."

The roar of a engine brought a luxury car fast through the iron gate beside the airport. Dr. Ernest in his first attempt to use this super car is very smooth. This breach has sounded the alarm. Soldiers climbed into jeeps to stop us.

"We're there! Heading for the runway!"

"But they're about to take off!"

"Just do it, Doctor!" I shouted with Jesie simultaneously.

"Okay! Okay! Stop yelling at me!" Dr. Ernest drove agilely avoiding one by one the pursuers who tried to crash his vehicle into us. Not so smooth drifting, but dr. Ernest did it.

"What are they doing? Stop the car before they reach the runway!"

"Sir, they are in front of us."

"Use full power to take off! Run them over if necessary!" The pilots push the plane's power until they increase the speed for the plane to take off. Our car had almost arrived when the plane started moving and we passed them followed by turning around 180 degrees to chase the plane from behind.

Of course at this time there were no pursuit cars trying to chase us from the front as that would hinder the plane from taking off.

"Open the roof!" Jesie opened the roof of the car according to my signal.

"We're going to get on this plane and dr. Ernest... I leave your escape wherever you like!"

"What? You guys will leave me alone? What kind of bullshit is this? You can't leave me here!" in the midst of grumbling dr. Ernest didn't realize that we had reached the rear tires of the plane that was about to take off and immediately left dr. Ernest without listening to him back.

"Hey! Hey!" Dr. Ernest realized that he was about to hit the other side of the runway, he swiftly turned the car around and looked for his own way out.

Me and Jesie have found a safe position to hide in the smallest place in the wheel storage section of the plane. Once the wheel doors closed and the tires stopped rolling, it was time for us to go after Sean and save John.

The roar of the engines was deafening the whole time Jesie and I intruded the plane from the wheel locker bay. The roar of this engine I will no doubt experience because this military cargo plane is very large. However, the buffer room we entered was only the size of one adult. I know I should go in first, but something stops me.

"We're going to get in from here and crawl all the way to the cargo hold."

"Is it going to be easy?"

"Not really, because of the cargo plane's large specifications for shelter, we have to crawl in this narrow space."

"Do you think I'll fit in?"

"Based on the shape of your body... hm... no problem," she said turning around after sizing me up with the gap we were about to enter.

"I'll go in first, don't bump into me from behind! If I move, then you may move, okay!"

"You're the boss," I replied ready to follow her directions. Jesie started crawling into the empty space which we took advantage of to get up to the cargo hold. After Jesie's feet entered completely into the gap, I also started to catch up with her. It isn't as easy as I thought it will be to crawl in a narrow place like this. I couldn't use my legs to move forward because it is so narrow. I can only hope with my hands to move little by little. Apart from being cramped, the sound of the engine is also very uncomfortable, even those that are what surprised me was that I couldn't see ahead. 'Jesie, you are too dangerous with your position even though you carry a bag. I'm a man after all, can this be over soon?' was how I muttered to this feeling of discomfort to avoid looking at Jesie's 'backside'. After moving for a while, Jesie's feet didn't seem to move. I immediately responded that she was not moving from her position. I had to look at her and Jesie signaled that there was a turn ahead. My head is starting to lose my mind thinking about how I turn in this narrow gap. Jesie deftly moved and put aside her posture then turned swiftly. I'm starting to think she's better suited to be a snake than a spy. I tried to imitate the movement, it's still not as easy as what I saw when Jesie did it. It's like my waist is stuck in this bend and can't go through it. I see Jesie's lip movement that seemed to mock me 'What's wrong with you? You just have to turn your body a little more!' Her advice was very useful for me and I was able to get through the intersection. Jesie arrived at a position where she could stand. I feel relieved that my suffering will end soon.

Jesie tried to open the cover that was in front of us. Her hands were very nimble to open the bolt with the small tool she is holding. Jesie put the bolt out of our reach so that no suspicious sound would be heard by anyone. I try to get into a comfortable position after seeing Jesie open the slit cover, but she closed it in a hurry and got back into position. This situation is awkward when the two of us are pressed against each other. This rather slender place becomes quite cramped if two people occupy it.

"They're still active, we'd better wait here until we get the best chance."

"It's still more comfortable here than before, I guess it's fine. How long?"

"Four hours, maybe more."

"Agreed!"

"We need an element of surprise when we get out of here."

"I have a flashbang, taser and baton."

"Can I hold the baton?"

"Of course, I brought two."

"Oh okay."

Nearly four more hours passed, I can't really count the time exactly. Jesie occasionally glanced at the situation. Finally she felt safe after I watched her checking one by one the people in the cargo hold and the items tied up in the middle of the cargo hold.

"Okay, they are enjoying their sleep."

"How many are there?"

"Four people, six if you add two people from the pilot."

"Wait, the pilot can attack us?"

"Don't you know that this plane can be controlled automatically?"

"I haven't taken any airplane lessons yet."

"Typical Forensics."

"I'll put it on my list if we getting out alive."

"You take the key from the guy over there, beat one more guy and free John." I observed the person that Jesie pointed at.

"How about you?"

"Let's hope Director Sean doesn't shoot me first." Jessie took a deep breath and shook her head. I don't want her to take too many risks especially in front of John. She mumbled and I listened to her words.

"Stop stalling time and do your job!" muttered Jessie under her breath. Then Jesie began stealthily breaking open the floor of the cargo hold and throwing flash bombs. Everyone there who was still half asleep panicked at the thing that was rolling in their midst.

"Watch out!" the bomb exploded and hurt their eyes and ears. Flash bombs are indeed very effective for subduing enemies by surprise. They aren't going to move when Jesie and I entered the cargo hold by climbing from a small space in the floor. I quickly beat up the person hanging the key on his waist. He fainted and the man to my left grabbed his gun to shoot in desperation as his sight and hearing were impaired. I quickly stopped him from pressing the trigger with a baton and hit him on the wrist until he let go of the gun and grabbed him before he fell. I used the gun to hit his face and head. On the side Jesie was about to hit the head of the first soldier but instinctively he caught Jesie's hand and stopped his attack. Jesie cleverly took advantage of the split second gap by electrocuting him with a taser until the person was electrocuted without moving. The next soldier who took his gun chased Jesie as fast as she could and wrapped his legs around the soldier's neck then she hit the bottom of the baton on the soldier's head many times until he fell. Before the soldier fell from his feet, Jesie did a backflip so that he wouldn't fall with the soldier. What a very interesting fighting style that only mercenaries can pull off.

I immediately unlocked John's bars and I released him along with the handcuffs. We're going to arrest Sean, but the pilot door opens and one of them trying to shoots me and John.

'Bang! 'Bang! Jesie used the soldier's gun to shoot the pilot and the pilot who was still sitting in his seat.

"Stop you guys! Or I will shoot this bomb and blow us all up!" warning from Sean while showing the timer on the bomb for thirty minutes and steadily decreasing. Sean was still rubbing his sore eyes, but kept making sure that we didn't move from his spot.

"I can make history John. The fall of your country will be my momentum to become the next presidential candidate."

"You have too much ambition to profit from war, Director Sean. I did the right thing when I was assigned to watch over you." Jesie challenges Director Sean.

"Hit! You are the spy!"

"Stop this now, Sean! You can still get out of this."

"As long as you guys are here I won't be able to run. Of course I will finish you all off!" he said he was about to press the trigger of his gun, but the body of a dead pilot shifted the plane's lever forward so that the plane suddenly swooped down and startled our footing. Sean's reflex was holding on to the bench, but Sean's hand that was about to press the trigger of the gun shifted his hand so that the shot hit the cargo hold opening button. The cargo door opened causing all the air pressure to suck out including Sean's gun which was accidentally released because he was shocked. Jesie's fall not only changed the direction of the plane, she was pulled out of the way and had trouble getting a grip to withstand the drag of this low air pressure.

"John!" shouted Jesie who was getting pulled out of the plane.

"Oh my God, Jessie, hang on!" I chased Sean by closing the bomb and hitting him with batons, but he was very tough for someone older than me.

"You're never going to make it, Policeman!"

"Let's see who wakes up!" I slammed my head hard into Sean and he passed out instantly. John takes the bomb away from Sean. Jesie was getting mired until she was sucked out of the plane.

"Oh no!"

"Grant, help me use this!"

"I will save her! You reroute this plane, close the cargo hold and jump with a parachute!" I grabbed the parachute John was holding and headed for the open cargo ramp.

"How do I put it on?"

"Just put it on!" I left John with nothing but a parachute bag and jumped out of the plane.

John runs hastily and moves the pilot's body which was falling on the plane's lever. He stabilized it then rerouted the plane's autopilot towards the middle of the sea. John returned to the cargo hold parachute bag and strapped as best he could. He finally started to understand how to use it after going through the entire bag he had tied and fastened. John ran to the button of the cargo runway, pressed the button and ran out of the plane before the cargo door closed completely.

I, who had jumped a few moments before, felt my first free fall while locking my parachute bag. I had a hard time determining my position because my body's horizontal position made my body oscillate in the sky. I managed to get the lock on so it clicked and I'm pretty sure the band is in place. I lost Jesie who fell first. I searched for it until I saw a small dot of my eyes. I thought 'that's her' and positioned my body vertically to accelerate my fall.

Jesie fell resignedly, she knew that she couldn't save herself after falling from the plane without a parachute. Jesie felt sure that this was what she would get after what she had done before meeting John. John gave her a chance to escape and have a new identity, but in his mind it was only implied that one day what he did as an assassin would come to him. Amidst Jesie's despair about her life being about to end, I emerged who chased her little by little from a distance. I patiently waited until I would be five meters away from him. When the time came, I positioned myself horizontally again to balance my falling speed with Jesie.

Even with a small distance, I need effort to catch it. Luckily Jesie understood my situation and our hands grabbed each other. I hugged her and opened my parachute rope. The first jolt surprised me because our weight was caught by the wide open parachute. But I'm relieved to know that we won't die after falling from the plane. John sees us from above and opened his parachute. The timing was very precise when his parachute inflated, he got a position next to us.

"How is it Ruchester finest, fun, isn't it?" I laughed at his conclusion to our story so far with what John promised me to skip classes at work.

"Whops, sea surface is getting closer." The descent using this parachute without realizing it was already getting closer to the sea surface under my feet.

"Release your parachutes!" Jesie's signal made me and John reflexively release our parachute bags and we fell from a height of eight meters. We fell in the middle of the ocean and immediately surfaced to take a breather.

"I mean take it off near the surface, you idiot!" John and I laughed at our own silliness. Not long after a patrol boat approached us and pulled us from the sea. I am relieved beforehand, but they suspected us because we are foreigners roaming in international waters.

"I told you, there are nukes that will be dumped here. We are not the criminals." I took hard to explain that we are not people from a foreign country crossing the international water zone.

"Don't panic, Grant, your way of explaining is so bad."

"Is there a better idea?" John pointed his finger up and all of us including the officer captured us up also looked up.

Sean started to regain consciousness after his head collided with mine. He who was still staggering felt the blood flowing from his head and saw that the plane was silent aside from the plane's engine. He remembered the bomb he was carrying and immediately chased it to carry out his plan. Sean opened the bomb cover and he saw the timer showing the countdown to ten seconds remaining.

"huh... I'm so fucked." The bomb exploded and emitted a red light explosion in the sky and startled the sea patrol officers. The three of us just enjoyed the explosion like a rare fireworks.

"Well, luckily it's all over." John is relieved that an officer is mysteriously taking calls. they hastily carried us away from the ocean.

In a luxurious, closed office, the three of us were facing Phill. It was him who freed us from officers who thought we were trespassers.

"Stupid! Stupid! Stupid! You're all stupid!"

"Don't get me wrong, I know you want to save the world, but that doesn't mean you can do everything on your own."

"Don't get yourself hurt, young master," he said softly to me. He didn't seem to dare to swear at me while the rest he said to John and Jesie. The door opens and enters dr. Ernest who was confused.

"Do you know how pain it is to get the four of you out by negotiating with the Greater Buturea government? I'm having a headache over your behavior today."

"Well sir, we saved the day, saved the world. What do we have to complain about?" explained Jessie.

"I thought you were dead, Jessica."

"No thanks to you."

"Go out there and make yourself useful."

"Yes, Sir!" Jesie left us, but she stopped in front of the door she had opened.

"Until next time, West Junior." John just turned his head to avoid meeting Jesie.

"Really? You won't talk to her? You won't know how much longer you will meet," said dr. Ernest gives advice to his best friend. John just kept silent, not wanting to respond to dr. Ernest's drama.

"So what do we do with Adrian?"

"We will convey to him, after all he is our client."

"Give him my regards."

"See you on the next case, Grant." John and dr. Ernest left us. I'm left with Phil who still has something to say to me.

"What are you doing, young master?"

"Involving John's case or something else? You have to be more specific."

"I don't think I need to explain in detail about what you did. But remember this…"

"One day you will become a target for others if you are constantly implicated by a problem that needs to be solved."

"Someone I've caught looks like no one can hold a grudge against me."

"I hope you will understand later, so please be more careful."

"Just like that?"

"A car has been prepared to take you home." I left Phill and accepted the offer to be driven home. What an amazing experience. I didn't really understand Phill's last message, but I felt he was telling me to be prepared for something that would try to knock me out of my actions of trying to uphold the truth. It is still a mystery as to what will come my way next.

================

CASE 3 – The Fallen

Caith and I are analyzing some data and samples. We are working hard as usual. Suddenly many people entered our room simultaneously bringing a very unpleasant situation to me. The evidence they showed me and said that I am the culprit. Eddie is trying to prevent these people from being tried for my crimes.

"This is impossible!"

"You must come with us, Mr. Dylan."

"Don't play around! Who are you people?"

"We're from the International Federal Bureau."

"What is the International Bureau doing in this place?" Eddie snapped loudly at the people trying to catch me.

"Mr. Dylan is arrested as a terrorist and a murderer.

....

We go back six days after I was dropped off at the Ruchester police force. It was late afternoon and I met Eddie who was getting ready to go home.

"Hi, Eddie." I greeted with a little bit guilty.

"Why do you look like you just had a fight?" I just chuckled and just nodded at him.

"Are you watching the news?"

"Yeah, right now there's been a lot of news about the big explosion in the sky..." Eddie suddenly woke up by seeing me in this state.

"Are you saying you had something to do with it?"

"I guess So." Eddie sighed. He felt that he could come home earlier today, but he didn't because of me. I just smiled a little at him and he replied by putting on a face mixed with worry and annoyance at me.

"I guess I'd like to sit somewhere else to listen to your story first and then I'll write up the report if necessary."

"Of course, I'm right behind you, Inspector." Eddie took me to walk to a diner. He decided to have dinner here after telling his daughter the news. Eddie still only sighed heavily and remained silent looking at me.

"What trouble did you done today?" a question Eddie was starting to remind me of Jesie's answer.

"Save the day, save the world."

"How did get involved with that matter?"

"It was John's client asking us to find out where his father went missing twenty years ago."

"You want me to believe that the missing persons case has something to do with the big ass explosion in the sky?"

"Because this missing person is a famous scientist named Hugo Rowland...," I said in a whisper so that no one else near me could hear.

"...and he still has the nuke he created."

"So that's what we all saw in the sky."

"The higher up of the agency in Greater Buturea, Director Sean, wanted the weapon to be detonated in this place and cause an imbalance in the country."

"Like war?"

"Yes! But we managed to stop it."

We talk a long story about how our investigation process started from infiltrating Aloysius II to get clues about Hugo's creation, then meeting the former marine who served as bodyguard for the deceased until we in Great Buturea met John's lover and underwent many actions after that. Eddie was silent, unable to enjoy his food when my story came to us jumping from the plane and landing in the middle of the ocean.

"Your story is truly the most valuable life experience."

"Is that what you're getting Eddie? 'most valuable life experience'."

"I'm just saying that not everyone gets the moment to do stuff like that."

"Fair point."

"Still, it's dangerous, Grant."

"I'm still alive, right?"

"Hmm... You make an active duty officer died in someone else's country. Someone will come after you."

"Fair warning. Someone said the same thing to me."

"You mean by 'someone; that is the man in all white who is often with you?"

"I think they'll help me get out of this."

"It's best if I tell this to the Captain tomorrow."

"Yeah, great idea."

"Is there anything else?"

"Nothing in particular when I got back to the office."

"Okay." Eddie finished his meal. We paid and left the diner.

"Go home Grant, don't let me hear you're in trouble again!"

"Very well, Inspector," I said before we parted ways. I immediately chased to the subway, back to my apartment. It feels like I haven't seen where I live in a long time. Even though it's not that special, I feel relieved to be able to feel the pleasure of lying on my bed. I just closed my eyes and my doorbell rang.

I opened the door and saw who it was. Tess was standing at my bedroom door with a small cloth-wrapped box in her hand.

"Hai, Tess."

"Hey Grant, are you busy?"

"Of course not, you want to come in?"

"Thank You."

"I just came back. You caught up with me very quickly."

"I followed you."

"What? Why?"

"Just worried." Tess patted my seemingly soiled clothes. I haven't changed my clothes yet. As soon as I got there I only thought of laying myself down and enjoying a relaxing rest until morning.

"Thank you, I'm fine. Do you mind sitting here while I change first?"

"Yes, please." I quickly grabbed my clothes and headed to the bathroom. Rinsing my face and drying it, changed my clothes and returned to find Tess who was opening the box she had wrapped in a cloth.

"Mind if I having dinner with you here?"

"Go ahead, make yourself at home." Tess opened the box and found she had brought me some food.

"I made it for you."

"It got me thinking, does your father know you're here?"

"He was the one who told me you were home."

"So?"

"I told him I wanted to bring you dinner."

"It's hard to believe he could let you meet me here."

"He knows, believe me."

"Well, let me have a taste of it." I took a mouthful and I found Tess' cooking delicious.

"How is it?"

"It was delicious."

"Really?" I just nodded and took her food again. We eat together, but don't engage in conversation. She seemed very happy to see me greedily eating the food she made. I still feel awkward about my previous mistake and I think this is the right time to talk about it.

"Are you still mad at me?" Tess just shook her head in her smile.

"I'm sorry I couldn't be around while you were looking forward to it."

"What are you saying, Grant? You are here now." She sounded fair with my circumstances.

"But I still owe you the 'date'. I'll make up for it, okay."

"All right, promise?"

"I promise." I don't know what this situation is like. It feels like being lit by fireworks. I don't really know about romance, but this just doesn't sound right. Tess was at my house and I tasted her cooking. I tried to reach her hand and she still had no reaction to refuse. I was startled by the sound of my cell phone ringing. The timing was so disturbing the mood.

"Why did your dad call me?" I picked up the call from him and tried to greet him.

"Are you guys done? I'm still waiting for her in the parking lot."

"What? Eddie..."

"What is it?"

"This is your dad, he's waiting for you in the parking lot," I said giving her my cell phone.

"Come on daddy, grow up!" I'm surprised Tess said that directly to her father. No wonder she let Tess come here since it wasn't even two hundred meters from his sights.

"...Okay." Tess handed me my cell phone and looked like she was saying goodbye.

"This is so much fun, thank you."

"I'll return your lunch box after I clean it."

"Does not matter. I'll take it. Bye, Grant." I opened the door and she expected our meeting more than this. I felt the responsibility to accompany her to the parking lot. It turned out that it was true that Eddie was waiting there.

"Thank God, you're back. Wait... why did he come with you?" said Eddie who had lost his boredom waiting for Tess.

"Thanks dad."

"I'm sorry, I'm just really bored here."

"All right... All right... Let's go home!" Tess got into the car and Eddie glared at me. I just shook my head as if to say 'nothing happened' and they left. I returned to my room and tried to finish the food Tess made and quickly rested.

This morning when I entered my room after a few days of not working. I saw Caith was busy doing his work. I thought I had come earlier.

"Caith, you early."

"Hey, look who wants to come to work today."

"Sorry about that."

"No problem, how was your vacation?"

"You can't really call it a vacation, but it sure is a nice place."

"I'd love to hear it, but can you help me with this and hand it to Eddie?"

"That's plenty! Did you work all night long?"

"No, Rip helped me. We pulled all-nighter to finish this."

"Now that's why you came early Caith, are you okay?"

"I'm still exhausted, but I can be more relieved to see you're here."

"Wait a minute I'll get this to Eddie." I rushed to bring the data file that Caith had finished working on and headed to Eddie's room. everyone there was shocked by what i brought including Eddie who just took off his jacket.

"There you go, detective."

"What in the world happened to you so early in the morning?"

"I'm just helping finish Caith's work, see you later." I hurriedly chased back to my room and followed what Caith would ask.

"Next?"

"Here, Grant." Caith gave me the next assignment. It's really not a matter of who is senior or junior, but me who has been behind for a few days with work makes Caith become in charge in this room. She is very dedicated with her work. All requests for examining data and the context of cases that she has traced are carried out appropriately and make reports. I also don't really know how much Caith has done assisted by Rip the amount of work, but when I'm here I will help with the work as soon as possible. It was noon and it seemed that all the reports had been submitted before they were due.

"Wow, Grant, you work so fast."

"Not really."

"Hey, guys. Would you like to have lunch?"

"Come in Rip, I ordered it for you guys."

"Really, Grant?" Catih was surprised to see that I had prepared everything for them.

"Of course, I promised, right? I'll take it downstairs in a moment." I met the delivery man and quickly brought it to Rip and Caith.

"Wow, Grant, I feel like I was given a special service from you today."

"Today is a special day, isn't it?"

"I want to feel this special day all the time, don't we, Rip?"

"He's very excited today."

"I feel energized after coming home from vacation."

"How are you feeling after the holidays?"

"I'd say that I seem to be enjoying more peaceful times like now." I told Caith and Rip about my adventures to Irepool and Great Buturea with consulting detective John West. A long story short that I went through with them not only experienced good things, but also experienced life or death situations when they knew that a dangerous bomb would explode and jumped from the plane. I couldn't tell from their expressions, who were just stunned by my story and actions, especially using Jesie's car and slipping through the tires of a military cargo plane. It felt like an embarrassment because it sounded like my story was showing off to them.

"If I was the one hanging there, I would have peed my pants," said Rip comparing myself to him.

"I can't believe what you're going through. I'm sorry, Grant."

"Don't be, I still feel bad leaving my job and giving you a heavy burden while I'm away."

"But compared to what you went through…"

"You should have seen him at the mob's gunpoint. He always stays calm going through it."

"I'm a planner Rip, my plans will fall apart if I panic."

"Listen to him. He is the best."

"Hey, what's behind your desk, Caith? Why the mess with the bullets?" My eyes fixated on the scattered objects behind Caith's desk.

"Oh, Rip, how many times have I told you not to put your toys in here."

"I'm sorry, I just finished making a test run of the Captain's order."

"What did you make?" I asked curiously.

"Last night while helping Caith with his reports, I also busied myself with these bullets."

"Feels light, what is it made of?"

"Rubber bullets, but designed to look like real bullets."

"It is great to make this with your own hands."

"The captain asked me to design and manufacture a non-lethal bullet type sample. This will help officers when they have difficulty making a choice to shoot."

"This is very good, Rip." Praise for his work.

"It has less weight, but it have same velocity as the actual bullet, so be careful with that thing, champ." Rip took the bullets I was holding and collected them in the box he had. Our preoccupation was a little distracted by the presence of officers knocking on my door.

"Grant, are you busy?"

"We just finished lunch, what's wrong?"

"The captain wants to see you. Caith, can you help me with this?" the officer said handing a file to Caith. I said goodbye by cleaning up our office. Caith immediately got to work and Rip carried his stuff outside.

"Why did the Captain call you at this time of the afternoon?"

"I don't know either, Rip."

"Oh, someone got in trouble."

"Thanks, Rip," I snapped at his taunt.

I parted ways with Rip and headed for Captain Briggs' room. I opened the room and I saw him having a discussion with someone I didn't know. He called me in and the mysterious guest remained unknown to me even though he turned his chair to see me.

"Mr. Dylan, I'm sorry to call you when you're busy. Do you mind if I ask a few things?"

"Of course, go ahead, Captain."

"Where did you go for a few days off work?"

"I was going to Irepool then the next day I'm going to Great Buturea."

"Why don't you apply for leave if you don't come to work?"

"I have urgent business, sir, I told Eddie on his first day off from work."

"I'm assuming your departure had good intentions, right?"

"Absolutely, Sir."

"Alright, I think that's enough from me, but my guest may have something else he wants to ask."

"Mr. Grant Dylan, am I right?"

"Yes, you are right, sir."

"Can you tell me, what are you doing in the Great Buturea Intelligence Bureau?" I was stunned at what this person knew. I looked at the captain and he gave me a nod. Looks like I have to answer this guy's question.

"We are looking for a dangerous weapon detected in the basement of the bureau."

"So you're saying that you entered our dungeon?" he said assuring me that he was indeed one of those in charge of the bureau. I feel more and more can not avoid it.

"Yes sir, you are right."

"How did you find a secret passage to the safest place in Great Buturea?"

"Someone told us the secret passage."

"Who told you?"

"Director Sean himself."

"He did?"

"Yes, Sir."

"Do you have any proof that he did?" I can only be silent to hide Jesie's involvement which they may not know about.

"I can't give you that information, sir."

"You infiltrated the place where the intelligence in Great Buturea is placed, took the nightshade and detonated it in the sky. I think I'm entitled enough to that information."

"I'm very sorry sir, I can't say anything until the news will be clearly stated in the public."

"You arrogant young man! You dare belittle us by withholding information." Captain Briggs immediately intervened in our conversation in a calm manner.

"Mr. Maximoff, with all due respect, our personnel would not do anything if it weren't for a good thing."

"How can you be sure, Captain? Your men might get out of control!"

"Thank you for coming, sir. Maybe next time we can continue this conversation."

"You will regret it, Captain!"

"Are you threatening me?" I felt a chilling rise from Captain Brigss as he stood up to politely invite his guest out, but that goodwill was met with threats from his guest. This silent tension sent chills down on my spine for a moment. Thinking back, I've never seen a captain this scary. He is very friendly, intelligent in managing his men, commends their work, and gives the right direction in carrying out the task. The best leader I've ever met. His irritation with the guest was like he didn't like it when his force was disturbed, especially by foreigners. Hearing the captain's voice suddenly deep with threat, the visitor tried not to anger the captain any further.

"I think that's enough for today, thank you for letting me interview your men, Captain." Maximoff rose from his chair and shook hands with captain. I expected him to be out of the room soon, but he stopped near me and looked back into the captain's face.

"You should have let him go, Captain. This man is too risky to be able to act beyond his means."

"I bet he'll be fine, sir. Officer Oliver, please escort my guest outside." Officer Oliver happened to pass through captain's quarters door and ushered the visiting captain out of the force. Captain still wants my presence to explain things to him.

"All right, Grant. how did you get involved in Greater Buturea?"

"I apologize, sir. I got involve too far on John's case which unexpectedly had a very complicated situation."

"John? You mean a private detective when you and Eddie were in Waywell?" I nodded.

"Did you hear about him too? Yes, that's right, sir." Captain Briggs just nodded his head listening to my explanation just now.

"Did you learn anything from him?"

"Yes, sir, John West has extraordinary deduction skills."

"I'm really looking forward to you having that ability one day."

"Excuse me, sir, is that what we're talking about now?"

"Oh, yes, back to our main issue. I'm sure you're tired from standing, why don't you sit down?"

"Thank you sir." Suddenly there was a knock on the door and Eddie entered the room.

"You called me, sir?"

"Right on time! Please, sit." I wonder what Eddie brought in that folder.

"Let's sum up the matter brought up by the Great Buturea bureau."

"Here they mention in the report that three men and one woman who were caught on CCTV infiltrated their underground." Eddie showed us a folder.

"Are there any damage reports?"

"Damage to the restaurant building, injured soldiers, several accidents that occurred on the highway and a breach into the military base," Eddie explained, looking at me as if to say I was a 'rogue'.

"Is there anything you can explain to us about that?"

"They know that we know red mercury as a raw material for nightshade. They realized that it was hidden in their basement and they arranged everything for us to find it and used Jesie as a go-between to set us up."

"You've been caught, how can you escape?"

"Director Sean is – was the one who originally said he would deport us changed his plans by executing us. He just needed to bring John. Luckily we were saved by Jesie, she stopped the executors by shooting them at a non-fatal point."

"I think that explains a lot about the reports of injured soldiers."

"I tell you guys, what we did was not an order from anyone, but we believe that stopping nightshade is the right way."

"I trust Grant, sir." Eddie tried to defend me.

"Now, dealing with the pressured matter on our hands will require a lot of help. Grant, I advise you not to get involved with anything during your off hours," suggested the captain.

"Yes, sir!"

"Eddie, keep an eye on him while he's working outside."

"Yes, sir!" Eddie replied firmly.

"Get ready, gentlemen. We will have problems worse than a murder case."

"Which is?" asked Eddie curiously.

"Political bureaucracy. We have to win this even if it takes a long time."

That afternoon after work hours, I had contacted Phill to meet me. Phill replied in a text message to meet at Bar Arandre. I finished all my work for today and hurriedly left the office. I tried to run as fast as I could to meet Phill. The only way I can get out of this problem is with his help. I pushed open the heavy bar door and saw a quiet bar with a single customer. The bartender named Andrew was wiping his glass and looking at him.

"Welcome! It seems you are in such a hurry."

"Thank you Andrew. I want something fresh, please."

"Okay, coming right up, you've been awaited by the guests sitting there. Please," he said kindly by giving me a warm towel to wipe my sweat. I head over to where Phill sits while tidying myself up.

"Do you want me to get straight to the point or wait for you to speak first?"

I said spontaneously without further ado.

"I think I already told you. I remember said 'One day you will become someone else's target if you are constantly entangled by problems to solve.', right?"

"So what came to me today is just the beginning?"

"We have do what is best, believe me."

"Do better." Phill just sighed unable to fulfill my request.

"Do you know how difficult it is to negotiate with the general of the Great Buturea nation? They really don't care what happened, they want someone to be responsible for it, but they make sure it's not them."

"Are they kidding? Sean did! Ask Jesie to explain to them. They ask for proof, so give it to them."

"I can't give Jessica to help testify for you. I've pulled Jessica from the Great Buturea. It's too dangerous to let her in their bureau.

"My God," I said sounding like I had given up. Andrew gave me the drink I ordered to calm my mind and tiredness.

"Is there another way out?" I asked while enjoying my drink.

"I assure you there is an only way, but you won't like it."

"Okay, what's the plan? It won't hurt if I hear it."

"Sorry about this, young master. You must be part of this organization. That's the only way," Phill's solution didn't sound simple considering how he knew my reaction to joining my father's secret agent organization. This wavering feeling engulfed me deeply and plunged me into confusion.

"Wow, you really know how to invite me to join when I can't be saved."

"We knew you would react this way, young master," he said confidently by looking at me.

"Fine, if you're serious about the only option, I'll think about it."

"Think wisely and make decisions quickly." Phill left me and I'm trying to think things over calmly.

I've ruined my life by dealing with the wrong country. I didn't even think it would turn out like this. If I hadn't heard what Phill had said before then I would have screamed as loud as I could and ended up in prison. I was still daydreaming for a while until I was startled by a tap on my shoulder.

"Eddie?" I was surprised by his presence.

"You're not your usual self, daydreaming in this place."

"Is it so? Why are you here by the way?"

"I happened to be passing by and saw this guy in a white suit coming out of a bar and driving a car. So, I have a feeling you're here."

"Sorry about that, I seem to be having a hard time after meeting the people from the Great Buturea bureau." Eddie took his position to sit across from me. Andrew also came to bring some whiskey with ice.

"Hey, whatever is weighing on my mind, you can tell me about it."

"This is much harder than I expected, Eddie. I wish I could tell you."

"Surprise me." Eddie insisted on making himself a listener of my problems. I sighed and tried to stay calm before giving him a chance to hear what I was thinking.

"For starters, my father owns the agency of the man in all-white suit you saw earlier."

"No Shit! Wow... you hit me from the start of your story. I've always wondered how you knew the men-in-white-suit."

"At the end of the pill suicide case, my father came to see me and asked me to join him."

"What's your answer?"

"Of course I refuse," I replied quickly.

"Is there a problem if you are together with your father?"

"I just still hate him who was never in my life."

"Tough love?"

"That's how he is. I hardly knew him all my life, suddenly he comes to take what I have earned." I told Eddie about my past. It's nice to have someone else willing to listen to what I've been through so far. Eddie was just so shocked by this history I was going through that he not only overheard, but made suggestions for me to investigate my foster mother's death. Of course I explained to him why I was seeing the consulting detective that I ended up getting involved in his case.

"Hey, look at the time. Looks like we talked late into the night." I looked at Andrew and he just gave me a nod. The nod is a sign that your bill payment has been paid off. I bet Phill did that. Eddie was still confused by me continuing to ask him out even though he wanted to pay for his earlier drink. I told him that it is done deal but Eddie had to invite me to dinner, of course to continue the story earlier and Eddie agreed to my request.

We walked to a place to eat which was not too far from Eddie's house. I also didn't forget that this diner was also like the place Tess and I enjoyed dinner together. It turns out that Eddie also liked this place when he took Tess with him when she was little. Our talk that had drifted away from its previous intention became a pleasant talk like father and son. I feel close to knowing about Eddie's youth and how he took care of Tess as a child because her mother died of cancer. The fun of our story was surprised by the presence of Tess who was already next to us.

"Wow... I can't believe what I'm seeing. You two seems are very close."

"Tess, how long have you been here?" his father said in shock.

"I was knocking on the window next to you and you didn't see me at all."

"Err… that… looks like we were too drowned in chatting and not looking around," I said and Eddie quickly made a seat for Tess. I knew he wouldn't let me sit next to her.

"I'm glad to see you, Dad, you've wanted to talk nicely to Grant."

"He's not at his best state right now, that's why I'm accompanying him."

"Something happened at the office, Grant?" Of course I knew Eddie was giving me a sign from his face to keep it a secret from his daughter. I really understand that his daughter can't be involved with the serious problem I am facing.

"I just had a bit of a fight with Officer Oliver about this year's Gridlock championship."

"What kind of championship is that?"

"It's a fast eating contest, baby girl."

"Someone got into a fight over an eating contest?"

"Err... Officer Oliver sure has a high temper and is competitive. He hated Grant after his first debut last year."

"Don't worry, I'll stay calm about it."

"Yeah, I was just making sure Grant here wasn't offended by what he said?"

"Do I feel offended here?" I asked innocently what Eddie was planning what

I didn't know.

"Shut up, Grant!" Tess and I laughed together as we continued our stories and ate together. I followed them home because Tess asked me to. Eddie just shook his head thinking about what he should do when his daughter was with the person she liked right near her.

"Father, thank you for today. You were very good to Grant."

"I'm just doing what I can," Eddie said, stretching his tie a little wider.

"Oh, Father, I love you both."

"Baby girl, can I have a minute with Grant?"

"Of course." I guess it's time.

"Hey Grant, about today that you mentioned earlier, can I explain it to Captain?"

"I don't see any problem in telling it, fine, go ahead."

"Okay, I'll tell him tomorrow. You need to rest, you need time to think about your options."

"I will think about it carefully."

"No, that was your cue to go home." I chuckled not knowing what Eddie meant to me. I just gave Tess a wave of my hand if I had the chance to meet again tomorrow or some other day. I left them and walked to my apartment. There remains a choice that is very difficult to make, but

I have made preparations to bring up a new choice and hopefully I'm not too late to make my decision.

On the way using the subway this morning I felt that I was being watched closely. I can't tell who is stalking my every move. This uncomfortable feeling makes me more alert when I'm on the subway or leaving the station.

"Grant!"

"Oh my God, Tess. You just startled me."

"What happened to you? I called you many times and you didn't see me."

"Did I?"

"Yeah, I called you from a block earlier and still didn't see me. You didn't cross the street to the coffee shop either. Are you all right?"

"I think I'm fine, can we go there?"

"Let's go!" Tess held my hand cheerfully and we crossed the road to a coffee shop. The difference is today I didn't order to-go. Just want to sit here relaxing until work time arrives. It turned out that Tess had thought the same way as I had already taken a seat at the table closest to the back door.

"It's nice to be able to change pace for an early morning once in a while, isn't it?" Tess said putting down her coffee and sitting across from me.

"This is really surprising. I didn't think you'd stop here before work."

"I just had trouble sleeping last night, Grant. I wanted to start this morning early to calm myself down with a cup of coffee before going to work."

"What a coincidence, I also thought the same thing this morning."

"Thoughts that made you statued like earlier? I still remember your face shocked when I startled you."

"That was my goofy face, please forget about it." I said while smiling teasingly at her.

"But it looked really cute, believe me."

"I believe you." We sipped coffee and kept talking lightly about last night when I was with his father. She was so happy not only to get along with him, but also get along with his father. Our conversation seemed to be coming to an end when I looked at the clock on the wall and Tess glanced at her cellphone screen.

"It's almost time. Can we get to work?"

"Yes, Grant. My editor has also notified me to see him."

"First time in the morning?" I asked as I got up from my chair and together walked out of the coffee shop with Tess.

"Yes, he said to meet him this morning for an errand."

"Good luck with your work."

"Thank You." Before we knew it, we had arrived in front of Tess' office.

"Have a nice day."

"You too Grant," he smiled and Tess entered his office. I also walked to my office.

In a moment I entered my room. My eyes were fixed on captain's room seeing Eddie and captain having a conversation. I might have guessed that Eddie was keeping his promise to discuss with the captain my concerns yesterday. Arriving at my room I saw Caith who had just hung up his jacket.

"Good morning, Grant," said Caith who was a little surprised by my presence after I knocked on the door.

"Good morning."

"Were you able to rest last night?"

"Yeah, how about you?"

"I can sleep better after work is done thanks to your help."

"I only did the ending. You do the hard part yourself."

"Thank you, I like your compliment."

"How about Rip?"

"What about him?" I saw Caith's face without the slightest emotion asking me that.

"Ah... sorry if I asked that. I thought you and Rip..."

"What's wrong with us?"

"You know, man attracted to women stuff." I explained unsure as to what I meant did happen to them.

"Don't exaggerate it, Grant. We're just friends."

"Really? Kind of dull, isn't it?"

"What makes you think that?"

"I just... saw how you two talked and looked at each other."

"Did you hear that Rip?" I was really surprised that Rip was already in this room and listening to what we were talking about.

"Sorry."

"You promised me not to tell anyone."

"This is Grant we're talking about. He's smart, he'd know it without me telling him. plus, he is also my friend."

"And my co-worker."

"Whoa... wait a minute, I don't understand what's going on here."

"Do you want to tell him or should I?"

"What happened to your long hair, Rip? Looks messy." I saw Rip busy fixing his hair.

"We've been dating for two weeks, but I asked him not to tell anyone." Caith said with frowny face.

"So when I ask you that it's as if Rip already told me. Is that what you're annoyed about right now, Caith?"

"Because in the last few days Rip said he wanted to tell you and I said no."

"Does it really bother you guys if you tell me?" I whispered to Rip.

"No dude. We're friends, right?"

"To be honest, I myself don't feel any awkwardness between the three of us."

"Really, Grant?" Caith spontaneously looks happy.

"Of course! What do you think the worst will happen if I find out about your relationship?"

"If my work performance is bad, you can just report directly to the captain. You know, you're close to him. I don't want to lose my job." I was silent at the expression of Caith who saw myself like what she said.

"It hurts, Caith. I still feel grateful for you helping me when I skipped work."

"Do you really mean it?"

"Yes, this time let it be my turn to help you... you two."

"Let's decide that only you may find out."

"Yes!! Isn't that great, Rip?"

"Thank you Grant." a knock on the door startled our joy. Eddie knocked on the door and was amazed at what had happened in our room.

"Feels like a beautiful happy day you three have here."

"I'm sorry, what's the matter, Inspector?"

"I asked you to come with me to the crime scene. Are you ready to do it?"

"I was born to be ready."

"Good, prepare your things! We're leaving in eight minutes."

"I will be there."

"Another case, feels good." Caith cheered me on.

"You've been weirder about crime cases lately." Rip teased me for being infatuated with crime cases.

"Crime cases make me work more." I immediately prepared my tools to work as a forensic at the crime scene. This feeling of joy is not because I am happy because there is case, but when my thoughts are bad it will feel better if I switch to work that requires more focus.

"I guess I should head back to my lab too."

"Have a good work, guys."

I caught up with Eddie who was already in his car. He shifted the car into gear and drove leisurely through the less hectic traffic.

"Is there anything I can find out before heading to the crime scene?"

"Before that, would you mind listening to my explanation for a moment?"

"Sure, what's wrong Eddie?"

"I've spoken to the captain."

"Oh, yes... sorry I already knew when I entered the office and saw you in his room."

"Let me finish."

"OK."

"Captain himself would be hard-pressed to help you out of your troubles. He has tried to use all his connections to help you, but they all turned their backs when it came to the Great Buturea government."

"So what's he going to do?"

"He tried his best to protect you for the time being. He said you shouldn't be very active outside of any country so as not to cause more dissension."

"Then what do you think?"

"He's on our side, Grant, and so am I. However, we will find it difficult if we act alone, we also have rules that bind us."

"I know you've done your best and I thank you for that. Therefore I'm happy to be able to work as usual again, helping you at the crime scene, right?"

"You're right, but I still haven't backed down from your troubles. I also need some time to think about my next plan." Eddie looked really serious about helping me.

"So, where are we going?"

"Ah... right. We will head to a small laboratory in this town."

"Alpha Lab?"

"Yeah, didn't you hear anything last night?"

"No, I didn't watch the news last night at all."

"What an easy your life as a cop is." Eddie shook his head and he still didn't continue his explanation until he got to the Alpha Lab.

"Is this what happened last night?"

"Yes, this laboratory burned down."

"I don't mind checking, but isn't the security tape go through Rip?"

"I told him to come with..."

"Sorry guys, Huft... Man, my hair really doesn't work together today." Rip was right on time when we said his name, he came with his hair neater than the one I saw earlier.

"...And here he is." Eddie finished his sentence after Rip caught up with us.

"Is this the famous Alpha Laboratory? This is the first time I can inside," said Rip admiring his dream laboratory.

"By now part of the lab is gone."

"Is it safe to go in there?" Eddie asked a firefighter who had just come out of the building.

"So far so good, sir. All flammable chemicals have been removed from this location. There's no air pollution either, that's good news."

"Alright, we'll go in to have a look around quick."

"This way, sir." The police officers entered first and then we followed them.

We followed the steps of the police and examined the condition of the building that had just caught fire. I haven't found anything that I can use to locate the source of the fire. Floor by floor we explore slowly and carefully. Our silence was interrupted in a fourth floor where Rip suddenly raised his voice.

"Ooh... My God!" he said after flashing something jet-black and sat up and another body sprawled out.

"We need an autopsy team!" Eddie said over the officer's radio.

A moment later the autopsy team cleaned up the body and gave it a marker of its position when it died. Rip was still out of breath trying to forget what he saw.

"Goodness gracious, Rip, you're not a kid anymore."

"I just... have a hard time forgetting scary things that will disturb my sleep later."

"What's wrong with young man these days?" Eddie asked me.

"Beats me!" I said that I do not know anything about the changing ages.

"That includes you too Grant, I can't imagine myself being your age."

"Embrace that change inspector, my genius little brain just can't forget what

I spontaneously remember," said Rip proudly to himself.

"Alright, let's find something that can serve as a clue to this case." We split up looking for anything we could find in this burning room. The news from the firefighters stated that the fire occurred due to malfunction in building pipeline which then the fire spread quickly towards flammable chemicals.

"By the way, what are they making here?"

"Are you kidding me, Grant?"

"Eh..? Do I have to know what they are doing here?"

"They make anything that can be used for many people."

"Revolutionary science to end hunger and equality, isn't it?"

"Exactly right! Wait, how come you already know? Didn't you ask me?"

"Sorry about that." I can't tell Rip that I just got a glimpse of what they're creating. That thing looks like a grain of rice. I admit that in this city it is not really a main staple, but in some developing countries or other poor countries it takes a very hard effort to grow rice so that it becomes rice as a staple food. Of course this rice is not something new, instead they are trying to create rice that can grow anywhere. It could change world history by eliminating hunger. Someone covered up this discovery by destroying everything they made. Too bad, there's nothing to save from what they're working on.

"Hey, look at this!" We went to Rip and saw what he found.

"Did you find the security camera?"

"A broken security camera." Eddie corrected my statement.

"But Eddie, this version has memory card in it. I can access it and with some luck I can get a glimpse of it moments before it breaks."

"By 'luck'?" I confused.

"Yes, what I mean by luck is a genius who is not appreciated."

"I leave that task to you." I threw the noble task of a genius to Rip while I was still busy looking around this place.

"So, is there anything else we can see here?"

Rip exited the building in a hurry and hailed a taxi to take him to Ruchester headquarters. We out of the building and take breathe a fresh air from before with a musty room with burnt marks that had been flushed out by the fire department.

"So what are you going to do now, Eddie?"

"I'm going to find some witnesses who were working here last night and had already gone home before the incident happened."

"You don't need me to accompany you, do you?"

"I'll do it myself, go back to force."

"Okay, I'll help Rip and Caith."

"See you again."

I returned to my office, I saw that Caith was already busy with the data and evidence that the officer had brought to our room. I sighed at the sight of this stuff being too much to bring all of it to my table. I checked them one by one and recorded the amount. While looking at what was in the burnt laboratory, we also waited for Rip's progress in getting the final footage from the security camera.

Time passed it was already dusk, the sound of heavy footsteps running toward us.

"I got it!" shouted Rip with a small item that he showed. That's the memory card I think of the camera that burned earlier.

"Did you recovered the data?" I said welcoming him.

"Here it is." Rip shows a mircoSD taken using tweezers.

"This thing has been cleaned up, but there is still some damage."

"Then let's take a look at this together."" I put the tape down and watched it with Rip and Caith.

"Here we go." We looked at the footage that the image is really broken.

"It's too badly damaged, Rip."

"We can only see two people having a conversation."

"Sorry... This is all I can do for the footage."

"Wait a minute, as far as I remember, apart from the camera, audio and motion sensors were also installed on the camera, right?"

"Yeah, if we could use the motion sensor to clamp the lips and the remaining audio..." I fiddled with the audio settings to boost the sound waves then mapped the lip movements of the broken record then cleaned up the image and voila! the image of about seventy five percent I have restored.

"Ta-da, and you're welcome!"

"You can show your magic too, Grant?"

"I can only improve the image quality with the sound and motion sensors he has."

"Again, let's watch the footage." I restarted the tape and saw two people who knew each other arguing. One of them wearing a lab coat tried to calm the person carrying the grenade. Their conversation took place and the grenade exploded in the man's hand.

"I can't guess what kind of problem they mentioned here."

"The grenade carrier said 'calling' him who did he mean?"

"I tried to roll back... here! He had the grenade pin removed by the time this tape was recovered."

"What about that?"

"That means, Caith, the bomber did believe he was going to die there. He doesn't want something, but wants to blow something up."

"But what is his purpose?"

"Well, the important thing is we report to Eddie first." Rip and Caith helped me make a report on the contents of this tape and we provided our respective conclusions and prepared them in the report. I let them go home first and still saw Eddie working at his desk. I went to him and handed him the file.

"Working overtime, Inspector?"

"Yes, I have a lot of witness reports that I need to sort back."

"It seems time consuming."

"How about you? Your cooperation is extraordinary in being able to restore the broken camera."

"It was burnt, Inspector."

"Whatever, what you guys have made is really great."

"Inspector... I mean Eddie, may I talk to you about something?" Eddie saw me and put off his work while I sat at his desk ready to listen to me.

"What do you think if my situation gets more complicated?"

"I don't want you to tell me to imagine that."

"..."

"All I know is you will make your best decision, whatever it may be."

"Even if it's a decision like my holiday at Iriepool?"

"Which decision was it? Blow yourself up on a train or free-fall from a plane?"

"Well... Technically, I jumped from a plane that came from Greater Buturea, not Iriepool."

"Those are the only two things I know you do crazy things about." He laughed.

"Okay, thanks for the advice. Good evening, Inspector."

"Good night, Brawler, see you tomorrow." I left Eddie still working and I headed back to my apartment.

Two days later after the investigation into arson at the Alpha Lab. Eddie's still keeping me busy with other cases. This time he took me on a murder case in a car parking on the docks.

"What do we have here?"

"A car with lots of bloodstains all over it."

"Where's the body?"

"Nobody saw it. Witnesses reported wanting to see the sunrise and they found this bloodstained car."

"Hm... any ideas whose car this is?"

"She owns it, Mrs. Palmer."

"I want this blood sample brought to Caith's room ASAP." I told the officers and they left with the evidence I gave them.

"I assume you've asked him, Inspector." I was still busy looking for traces that I might be able to get in the car, it turned out to be only a business card that said Lifeat, an insurance company.

"Said her husband was driving to rest his mind, a habit of his husband."

"Hmm..."

"Anything so far?"

"I have four ideas, but I have to meet the person in charge of taking care of the victim's life insurance." I showed Eddie this business card and we went together to meet him.

When we arrived at a Lifeat insurance office, we met Mr. Janus and Eddie start asking questions about Mr. Palmers.

"That was so unfortunate, he was one of the founders of this company."

"Is there anything you know about him lately?"

"I only know when he retired as a director in this company, then he had a lot of debt and was depressed about his retirement days," said Mr. Janus while scratching his arm.

"Is this him?" I asked showing a photo of someone hanging in the room behind Mr. Janus chair. Mr. Janus turned his chair around and saw what I was pointing at.

"No, it's Mr. Mustang. He was a first founder for all of us."

"Oh... Alright, forgive us. By the way Mr. Janus, do you have any change?"

"Huh?"

"I saw a cigarette vending machine accros the road and I think I want to buy one." I held out money to change him a dime. Mr. Janus took his wallet and looked at the bills he had.

"I'm sorry, I got no change."

"Ah... very well, thank you for your time Mr. Janus." I left him and Eddie hurriedly followed me.

"What was that, Grant? I haven't finished asking him yet."

"I have an idea of the case, Inspector. Meet me in my office."

"By the way I have change if you still want to smoke."

"I was only joking, Inspector. Don't worry about that, bye." I waved leaving Eddie. he is still full of question marks about what I have found about this case. We both went back to the office and Eddie followed me to our office.

I went to Caith who had received my request for a blood sample and it turned out that she had already tested it. I smiled and gave her appreciation for the results she had found. Of course I could have guessed before Caith checked. This time it was more certain because the blood left behind a bubble reaction after being dripped with a test liquid. Eddie was still gaping about what magic we were playing. He's trying to be the most ignorant in the world by trying to listen what I have to say.

"How much blood do you think was in that car?"

"As much blood in the human body?"

"No, just a pint."

"A pint?"

"Yes, Mr. Palmer donated a pint of his blood and it has been frozen."

"Frozen?"

"The sign that the blood is bubbling is like boiling. Those are the traits."

"So they just splashed the blood over here. Where is he now?"

"Gestasia."

"Wait a minute, how did you know?"

"I saw Mr. Janus, right on the neck and wrists like sunburn. Obviously that's not our climate here at this time of the month. Especially when I asked for change, I saw from his wallet sheets with foreign currency and change as well."

"So the car is just a set up?"

"You could say it's like insurance fraud."

"But, isn't Mr. Janus as the insurance agent?"

"Because he and Mrs. Palmer were the one who planned it."

"Mrs. Palmers?"

"Oh yeah, she is also involved. In short Mrs. Palmer made a pact with Mr. Janus to get rid of him as if his husband had been killed and hide him in Gestasia. She will receive a sum of money from life insurance and share it with Mr. Janus. So arrest them now, Inspector."

"I will, thanks, Grant." Eddie left me to do his job. I hear Caith's soft applause and she smiles at me.

"You really are amazing, Grant."

"Thank you." I said accepting his compliment by sitting in my chair.

"Hey, sorry if I brought this up again." Caith tries to strike up a conversation while I'm already seated.

"Don't mind about that."

"Excuse me?"

"You feel bad after hiding your relationship story from me. You don't think I'm not who you think I am, isn't that what you'd say, Caith?"

"What got into you today? It's like you can read my mind."

"It's hard to explain, why is that?"

"You are like a rare person who walks in the middle of a case and solves them one by one. How can I imagine what's on your mind."

I did as Caith suggested. Trying to get through the middle of a case and solve it as fast as I can. I just hang around during the day finding the puny criminal and arresting them on the spot. Prevent a robber trying to escape from the pawn shop. Meet Eddie again, who has brought two suspects who have confessed to their actions. It seems like today, time seems to pass very slowly and I enjoy all those activities. However, in my heart there is still a void that still needs to be filled. Apart from the threat the Great Buturea State has not yet come to face me which has prevented me from doing much.

Excess work today until the evening completing documents makes me very hungry. I headed for a diner that was farther and different because I didn't want to see Tess with my face like this. It looks more like a place for people to drink with a more dim atmosphere and not so many visitors, but some people are laughing while drinking beer. I tried to find a seat away from the reach of these drunkard. I ordered my drink and a french fries to fill my empty stomach. This place really isn't that bad if no one gets drunk. My instincts as a cop will make me work more during my non-working hours. That would be troublesome. I try to see everyone and also aware the direction of my exit if things happen that I don't really expected. I looked at my phone for a moment and tried to send text to Tess for a moment. Too bad I can't see her tonight. She seemed to be still busy with the work given by her superiors. I hope the busyness will pass quickly and I can hear the success stories. You know what? I miss her.

After my order arrived and I ate a few pieces of french fries, someone who came from out of nowhere joined me and sat in front of me.

"Are you a person whose face is familiar to me?" asked someone with a close-cropped haircut and picked up my dinner.

"Maybe you have the wrong person." I tried to dodge the question.

"I can't be wrong about this."

"Why do you say that?"

"Because... my superiors told me that you are a dangerous person."

"Where are you from?"

"I am a messenger from the Buturea Kingdom, buddy."

"Don't start 'buddy-buddy' with me, what do you want?" My instincts were warning me of danger with this person. Too dangerous especially with the knife in his hand.

"Oh, yes... Hm... I'm sure my boss said something. Ah, you will pay for what you've done!" he threatened me in a low voice, but full of confidence with a grin on his face then left me. Looks like he spilled salt near my food on purpose.

The next day when I arrived at the Ruchester Office when I met Eddie to report my work in the morning, I overheard Captain Briggs' voice from Eddie's room. It's rare for me to hear the captain's voice out of his room.

"The captain's room sure is noisy this morning."

"He had guests visiting him."

"I wonder who came to visit him."

"Officer Pearl told me his brother was coming."

"Captain's brother?" I tried glancing around the room and saw something I didn't expect. The person who made threats to me last night turned out to be Captain Briggs' younger brother.

"I've met him before, Eddie," I whispered to Eddie.

"No freakin' way, Captain Brigss told me earlier that he has brothers not from the same mother. That person is his half-brother."

"He met me yesterday at the bar and threatened me."

"Why on earth did he do that?"

"Because he's from Great Buturea." Eddie got up from his chair and saw the man. Apparently he just realized that his face does not look like people from this area.

"What did he say to you?"

"He delivered a message from his government that I will pay for what I've done." Captain came out of his door and called out to us. Of course Eddie and I were spontaneously surprised because he involved us at the same time as there were guests who were with him.

"Excuse me, Captain."

"Sorry to call you at a busy time, introduce my brother Leonard Briggs."

"Half-brother, we have different mothers."

"You're really going to say that?"

"That is a fact and the fact is that my brother is here hiding a top international fugitive in this peaceful base of his."

"Don't you start with that Leo."

"I became the top international fugitive?" I whispered to Eddie curiously.

"Not now, Grant." Eddie felt I was proud of the title, but I was surprised it wasn't heard anywhere.

"That's right. We will meet again, fugitive."

"Grant Dylan is one of my best officer. I won't let you catch him."

"We'll see that, brother Jerry," he said as he was about to get up from his seat.

"Thank you for the opportunity to visit, bro, but I reject your proposal. I have work to do."

"I'll catch you later!" as usual threats from Lenonard did not use harsh language or raise his voice. He threatened in a relaxed voice and had faith in what he was saying. I feel that he will be a troublesome person. He just left us without another word.

"Have my ears betrayed me? He just threatened Grant right in our faces."

"Please sit down, both of you."

"What's wrong with your brother, sir?"

"He still hasn't changed after these ten years, what a troublesome child."

"So how are we going now, captain?"

"Before we go there, Leo seemed to give a warning."

"Could you persuade him, Captain?"

"There's nothing I can do. I know Leo to be a stubborn kid especially when it comes to me."

"You seem to have a lot of bad memories with him."

"If you had a half-brother, Eddie, that would have happened to you too."

"Too much competition between him and you I'm guessing."

"You're right, Grant. I'm sorry that my own family is after you, it's also a difficult matter for you to avoid it."

"Describe him to me, Captain."

"He used to be a soldier, very intelligent, his ability can only be done by himself, he has a sharp instinct to complete his mission."

"Soldiers who get medals."

"It's very difficult if we try to distract him from the mission he's been given."

"Can you guess what he's planning, Grant?"

"Naturally, I have to die at his hands. Excuse me!"

Eddie followed me out of the room and tried to chase me. He was calling my name, but I didn't stop to hear him because I was lost in thought.

"Hey Grant! Slow down!" Eddie caught me by the shoulder and snapped me out of my thoughts.

"Sorry, I have to do something."

"You want to be killed by him? Don't jinx it!"

"Of course I don't want to die." I said and continued walking to my room. I got to my room at the same time as Eddie, but to our surprise Rip and Caith were arguing.

"Hey... Hey... what happened to you guys?" Eddie intervenes in their argument.

"Sorry, Inspector. we shouldn't be doing this at work."

"What's wrong with you guys? I often see you two eating together, why are you fighting now?"

"Quarrel over love." I sat back in my chair, ignoring what they were going to say and I started typing quickly on my keyboard.

"We just fought about Rip not finishing his work right away instead of coming to my place."

"Is that a matter of the Captain's request, Rip?"

"I've finished it. I'm only seeing Caith for a bit to rest my mind."

"You said you were too groggy in the middle of the night to think you weren't done."

"Hey, Never mind!" Eddie tries to stop their fight which resurfaces. An officer entered our room and called Eddie.

"Inspector, we have a murder case, you are requested to come to the scene as soon as possible."

"Fill me downstairs. Grant, you with me!" Eddie came down from our room to listen to a short explanation from the officer who gave him the information.

I was left temporarily to watch Rip and Caith argued.

"Rip, come here for a second," I called Rip so they wouldn't argued again, that's the only way I could think of.

"What design is this, Grant?"

"Can you make it in time?"

"You added a new property from the previous design, how about the approval of the Captain?"

"I just asked you to make one for me."

"Okay, I'll give it to you this afternoon."

"Thank you, Rip."

"Caith and Rip try to fight when I'm not around."

"Be careful there, Grant." I left them and headed out of the office and saw Eddie getting ready to leave. We didn't really talk and I don't think Eddie wanted to bring up my problem anymore, nor did Rip and Caith fight about it. Eddie also still couldn't stop thinking that a murder had occurred at a critical moment like this.

Arriving at the crime scene, I saw officers arguing with someone who is elderly. My head is starting to get dizzy why there should be fights everywhere.

We approached them and tried to listen. It turned out that the old man was the victim's family. He was asking the officers to look for someone who seemed suspicious to him, but the officers asked him to come to the police station for questioning.

"I told you he has short hair!"

"Please help us sir to identify the culprit in the office."

"I don't want to come to the office, he has short brown hair and is wearing a black T-shirt," he shouted at an officer. Eddie tried to keep them apart and took his time to question the old man.

"Excuse me, I'm an inspector from Ruchester, and you are?

"Eugene. Are you trying to play good cop on me, Inspector?"

"Calm down, try to tell us what happened, sir."

"For the past two days, my boy told me someone was stalking him."

"What time was it, sir?" Eddie tried to pull out his pocket notebook to jot down the old man's statement.

"I think he met me at eight in the evening."

"You have anything to prove that?"

"How could that be? I'm just an ordinary old man."

"But I see you as elderly and still look excellent even from me."

"I used to be in the navy, there's nothing wrong with me carrying on a better lifestyle than the average old man."

"All right, Mr. Eugene. Can you provide your address and phone number so we can contact you when needed?"

"So you're not going to catch the suspicious person?"

"We need you to describe the characteristics of that person so we can describe him to our APB (all-points bulletin)."

"Hey, young man, are you going to help me or the same as these cops?"

"He is a senior police officer, sir. I think you better follow his lead."

"So, what are you doing here, haircut?"

"I was working and saw the body seemed to have been attacked from behind and he couldn't say who did it because the culprit had left him

long   before
he tried to see who the culprit stabbed him. Two stabs in the back of his stomach and side thigh to make sure he can't move too far from his position. I can tell he's a man who really knows how to kill. Like ex-military or ex-navy."

"You arrogant bastard! You think I did it?"

"I didn't say you did it, you did."

"Calm down you two! He pointed out who did it and you also don't make deductions that offend other people."

"Let us work and if you can't work together to help us then let us do it ourselves."

"Tch!" the guy left us after he expressed his dislike for me. Eddie started asking me to judge by what was going on here.

"What is wrong with you to start a fight with that person?"

"He just wants to be heard but doesn't want to cooperate, I just have to get him out of here and try to find who the real culprit is."

"Short hair and black T-shirt, do you think he really is from here?"

"No, he made up this murder."

"You mean Eugene did it?"

"I'm telling you that the real culprit is make it looks like a usual robber."

"Why would he bother to do that?"

"Because he's been tagging this person for a few days."

"You can tell because?"

"He has a wallet and a fancy watch. A thief couldn't have missed this even though he knew that his fingerprints would be on it," I said as I handed the wallet to Eddie he hastily put on his gloves.

"You're right, he just missed this guy's precious treasure. He happened to have a lot of money with him and the killer just left it here."

"If we follow Mr. Eugene's story that someone has been stalking victim for the past two days. It would be better if he didn't act so paranoid about the police."

"Yes, I also wonder why former soldiers and police never got along."

"If you ask me Inspector, I once heard that story from an ex-Marine back in Iriepool. He opened up the story when he was retired and it was like the country didn't care about them anymore."

"Wow, so they are taking their frustrations out on people who are still actively working for the country."

"On the one hand, yes, maybe he wants to remind us that we will end up like them in the future."

"That makes sense."

"By the way did you see something around the corner of that building?" I turned my face to the alley that was in the shops two blocks from my position.

"I didn't see anything, why?"

"Someone is keeping eyes of this this place."

"Are you serious?"

"He is trying very hard to see if we can solve this case or not."

"Should we go after him?"

"Never mind, when I saw him earlier he immediately disappeared from that place."

"Is that all?" said Eddie as he accepted the last piece of evidence from me.

"Yup, we can already go back."

We're back during work hours. I immediately gave my analysis of the murder.

It does not feel that I finished my work until the evening. I tidy up my quiet room already, not even just the night shift. I returned to my apartment slowly and I also did not expect that I had arrived at my apartment. I opened my room door and found that my room seemed to have a slight change. At first glance it didn't seem like anything had moved, but my instinct was like a marker signaled danger. I tried to slowly explore my room. I began to realize that there seemed to be a smell that beckoned me to a window in my room. A box? I've never seen this before. I opened it slowly and saw that it contained a knife with bloodstains. I held it and my head showed a memory that this object was used to kill the victims at the crime scene earlier. Based on the drop of blood that was still left on this knife. I was startled by a body lying face down on the floor of my apartment. The police knocked on my apartment door and tried to open it. They were able to break in after getting help from the apartment owner to open the electronic lock.

"Grant Dylan, put down your knife and raise your hand."

"Who have you killed, Grant?"

"I don't know."

"Base, we found a body in Grant's apartment, requesting assistance to investigate the crime scene here!"

"Grant Dylan, you are a suspect in this murder! You have the right to remain silent. If you don't choose to remain silent, whatever you say can be used against you in court," said a policeman who handcuffed me and took me to the police station. I tried to stay calm and quickly thought of a way to get away from these false accusations.

That night I was immediately taken to Ruchester headquarters. Everyone was shocked to see me handcuffed. I didn't expect Eddie to be there. He seemed to be in such a rush to get here before I did.

"Grant!"

"Make way! We're taking in a murder suspect."

"Eddie, what happened?" Captain asked.

"Captain, Grant has been arrested on murder charges."

"How did it happen?"

"Hey, why did you catch Grant?"

"We found a body in his apartment, sir, we found him while holding this knife," said an officer while showing Eddie a knife that was in a plastic wrap as evidence.

"Give me the data in my room. I will ask him myself."

"I'm coming with you, Captain." Eddie followed Captain to his room and waited for the arrest filing from the officer. Thirty minutes later they were waiting while discussing the possibilities that might occur when the officer came to give the folder to the captain. Captain Briggs rushed into an interrogation room followed by Eddie. They headed for a room with translucent glass showing me in the middle of the room and my handcuffed hands on the table.

"Look at him, Eddie. How could that kid do this?"

"I can't believe he did it, sir."

"All of this confusion actually happened things beyond our expectations."

"Of course we will not give up, sir. Grant's fate depends on both of us."

"I hope you're right, Ed." Captain called Eddie his first name as if they were close friends. There is no rank while helping others who are subordinates he trusts. The captain knew very well that this was all a fabrication while looking at me who was still sitting still.

Of course from the inside of this room I see the window of the room like a mirror. However, this mirror is a two-way mirror where the outside can see the me inside. The door opened and in came Eddie and Captain Briggs to question me. I don't know whether my words can be trusted by them or not.

"How are you feeling, Grant?"

"Can we skip the pleasantries, Captain? I'm not the culprit."

"We are aware of that, but we have to do this by asking you. You must know about the procedure."

"Captain, you guys are wasting time, the real culprit is still on the run after he managed to frame me."

"Do you know who was stabbed to death in your apartment?"

"I know, sir."

"Who's he?"

"It was Mr. Eugene, sir."

"Where do you know him?"

"It was one afternoon that Eddie and I were working on a case and he was there."

"Are you insulting him?"

"Not to my knowledge."

"Fight with him?"

"What's the point of that question, Captain?"

"Here it was mentioned by the officer who was there that you had a fight with him, argued with him until he got annoyed with you."

"That incident to this question is completely irrelevant."

"Just answer it, Grant," Eddie said between me.

"I did mention it and he was mad at me because what I said made him feel like he was the culprit, but I never mentioned the accusations and he just jumped to his own conclusions."

"After that, did you see him again?"

"No, I'm busy working and giving the results of my analysis to Eddie."

"Yes, Captain, he handed me over at 7:10 p.m."

"I remember it seems like after that you received a call, right?"

"Yes, Sir."

"Then where did you go?"

"I went straight home, sir, no stopping or talking to anyone."

"Is there any proof?"

I sighed hearing the request for proof that at that time I didn't even stop anywhere and talk to anyone.

"Why don't you try asking Rip to access all the surveillance cameras I've passed? Maybe from there you can prove what I did."

"Thank you, I will do what you suggest."

"..."

"How Mr. Eugene can come into your apartment?"

"I don't know, I know i felt something was wrong when I walked into my apartment."

"Felt wrong how?"

"My head was pounding with my memories from before I left the apartment and something seemed to have happened before I entered my apartment room."

"What strange thing did you remember?"

"At first I couldn't feel it, after a while I smelled blood in my apartment."

"Then you approached where it was headed and found him dead in your apartment."

"Earlier I found a box that I don't know where it came from."

"You mean this box that contains the knife?" said the captain showing it.

"I swear I never saw that thing in my apartment."

"Judging from the shape it looks like something new. Are you sure no one has bought a new knife recently?"

"I'm pretty sure the kitchen equipment in my apartment is a bit old, but it's still in very good condition, so I don't think I need to replace another knife."

"We can confirm the truth. Furthermore..."

Question after question from Captain Briggs I answered quickly and left no doubt for him. I'm sure all my answers can be clarified that I'm not the real culprit. I occupied the room until morning. Eddie only gave me a cup of coffee and a piece of bread for breakfast. I am grateful that at that time he is on my side.

"You all right, Grant?"

"Don't worry, I can manage it."

"We still can't let you go, but your report already shows there is a deviation from the actual case."

"How long will it takes?"

"As long as it takes Rip and anyone else who is assisting the captain to ensure that your report is valid you are off of here."

"Who is this 'anyone else'?"

"Police officer, Grant."

"..."

"Is there something wrong?"

"The timing."

"What's with the timing?"

"Right after I opened the strange box containing the knife, the officers were ready with the owner to open the door at my apartment."

"What do you mean, Grant?"

"Someone told them I was already in my apartment."

"If that's true then the real culprit did arrange this murder as if you were the culprit."

"There's more, Eddie."

"Don't be... you're thinking too far, Grant."

"You just can't believe it's happening, Eddie. Our force was infiltrated by that person."

"You mean, there are enemies among us," said Eddie surprised. Suddenly Captain Briggs enters my room and startles Eddie.

"Good morning,"

"Morning, sir," me and Eddie said together

"You look tough, Grant."

"How's it going, Captain?"

"Looks like Rip saved you today and several officers have also provided evidence that you never bought the knife at that store."

"They found it?"

"Yes, the type of knife at the crime scene is a special brand, not all shops sell it. They showed a photo of you whether you had ever been to that place and all the employees there said they had never seen it and it was proven by their surveillance cameras."

"Isn't that great, Grant?"

"..."

"You don't seem as happy as I thought you were." Eddie was still confused by the look on my face and the opinion he couldn't express to captain. I just feel like it's too easy for me to prepare. The real culprit surely couldn't be that stupid to leave a way out for me to be free so quickly. I had to improve my planning to counter the setup he was about to prepare for me.

"Have all my charges been dropped?"

"Still in the press conference process. Can you wait a little longer? Then you go home and rest."

"I'm sorry, sir, I still have work to do."

"You didn't rest last night because of the arrest. Put your mind at ease and take the day off," Eddie pleaded.

Eddie took my handcuffs off after all the business was cleared up. I didn't heed Eddie's words to get some rest. I just wash my face and go back to my office. Eddie couldn't follow me because he didn't know what I was thinking. I entered my room and Rip and Caith were surprised to see me free from interrogation.

"Grant, are you all right?"

"A little sleepy, but I'm fine with this coffee." I said while showing the coffee

I brought.

"Why don't you just rest?"

"No, let me work." Caith and Rip just looked at each other couldn't do anything for me.

"Do something Rip."

"I've never seen him like this."

"What should we do?"

"I guess I should go first, see you later, Caith."

"Rip, is what I asked yesterday done?"

"Ah, yes… here it is." Rip gave me a magazine suitable for 9 mm pistols. I opened my cupboard and replaced the magazine on the gun I had. I tucked it in the back of my shirt and continued my work.

Caith and I are analyzing some data and samples. We are working hard as usual. Suddenly many people entered our room simultaneously bringing a very unpleasant situation to me. The evidence they showed me and said that I was the culprit. Eddie was trying to prevent these people from being tried for my crimes.

"This is impossible."

"You must come with us, Mr. Dylan."

"Don't play around! Who are you?"

"We're from the International Federal Bureau."

"What is the International Bureau doing in this place?" Eddie snapped loudly at the people trying to catch me.

"Mr. Dylan was arrested as a terrorist and a murderer."

"This is absolute nonsense!" Eddie shouted to my defense.

"Don't come into contact with the suspect or I will arrest you too! stay away!"

I was taken and left my room and led down the stairs with every officer in the lobby watching me.

The convoy of men carried me out of the Ruchester base. They took me to a prisoner's car. They didn't seem to realize what I had under my clothes because they rushed me from the office to avoid the tantrums of every officer as well as Eddie who tried to prevent me from being taken out of the headquarters.

"We're out of the Ruchester PD and ready to take the detainee to the airport."

"Use route two, stay alert."

"Yes, Commander," the conversation between International Federal Bureau officers I overheard on their radios.

"Take care of him!" said the officer who closed the door accompanied by providing four guards for me. They positioned two people sitting in front of me and to my left and right. This formation is very strategic in my opinion so that

I can't move against four people. The handcuffs on my hands were also one of the things that prevented me from defeating these four people. Right now I'm just massaging my right wrist down to the thumb. I did that slowly over and over again without the guards noticing. For them seems like I do that while praying that I can be saved from this problem and what they know is that I will not be able to escape from them.

Eddie is still confused about what happened in his office just now. One of his man was taken out carrying the label of a crime of terrorism which is still rife with the conflict with the Great Buturea government. However, Eddie still couldn't accept that they thought I was the culprit of the murder because they had confirmed the situation after interrogating me. Eddie and Captain Briggs still couldn't do anything about it. Captain

Briggs returns to his room to find a way to get Grant Dylan released from their charges. Eddie, who was left alone in the lobby, began to look for ways to provide assistance. Caith came to him and tried to call Eddie out of his reverie.

"Um... Inspector, do you have a moment?"

"What's wrong Caith?"

"I think Grant left us something." The two of them rushed back to Caith's office and Rip is at my desk looking through my computer.

"Can you explain to me what Grant said?"

"We were curious as to what he was doing before he was brought in by the bureau officers. At first I thought he was working on the results of a test we were working on together."

"So?"

"I asked Rip to reveal the password to unlock Grant's work one last time."

"It turns out he left a message for us."

"Let me see." Eddie leaned over to my computer screen and he saw a map.

"Where is the place he marked this?"

"A power generation facility at the northern end of the city of Bratginia. The location is in the direction of the airport he is likely going to."

"Why did Grant show me a map of this place?"

"He also gave a written message."

"You should have told me that before showing this map."

"Alright, my bad."

"Don't confuse the inspector, Rip." Rip showed Eddie my computer monitor.

"My God, Grant is in danger!"

Back again to my situation of being brought in this closed detention car. I couldn't even see the window outside. It felt like this trip was not very pleasant and it felt like it had been a long time in a vehicle that was not very comfortable. Their gazes were all still trying to intimidate me.

"Where are your guys coming from again?"

"International Federal Bureau."

"Really?" I chuckled.

"Just shut your mouth!"

"They are just intelligence agents, not executors."

"In your case, we make an exception."

"Wow... I'm flattered, man."

"One more word out of your mouth you will regret it."

"Here's one more word from me..." suddenly the car lost its balance due to a flat tire. They informed the driver of the vehicle who said that there was a sniper shooting at the tires of their car. Another tire explosion sounded and overturned the car. I took this opportunity to break my right thumb finger to break free from the handcuffs and beat all four of them. It really hurts. The screams as the truck rolled over not only gave me a chance to escape, but also knocked them off balance. Three of them had passed out after I hit them on their temples and lower jaws. Only one more person was still trying to take his gun to stop my recklessness, but I quickly grabbed the gun behind my shirt and fired one bullet right on his head.

I was thrown into the side of the ceiling of the vehicle. The position of the truck has been reversed. I couldn't open this heavy back door and wait for someone to open it from the outside. A surviving driver confirmed that the fugitive was still inside. He opened the door and was shocked to see that I was ready to aim the gun on his face. No one is trying to ambush me anymore. I ran into a power generation facility that was currently unattended. I walked into the grass to avoid being seen from the edge of the road. Someone quickly grabbed the gun that was in my hand.

"End of the line, Mr. Terrorist."

"Leonard, looks like you got my message."

"You are acting bold enough to call me to meet face to face here."

"I just want you to turn yourself in."

"On what grounds?"

"Don't play dumb, Leo! I know you killed Old Man Eugene because he knew your identity, right?"

"Also his foster son, don't forget about him."

"It seemed easy enough to make you confess."

"What can I say I'm very bored waiting for you to do something wrong," said Leonard who pointed the gun at me.

"So you're the one who arranged all these murders so that I become suspect."

"Of course, I uniformed my men and entered when you found him. Perfect timing, right?"

"Too perfect for me."

"It wasn't difficult for me to get the key to your apartment. I made the old man follow me and he came in to lunge at me to confess what I did."

"So you keep his mouth shut?"

"He was just a pawn I used to frame you. So, I suggest you return to your jail home."

"Or shoot me... kill me, now."

"Is this just sentimental or have you given up so quickly. I'm disappointed in you, Grant."

"We stand here a little longer, I'm sure you will regret it."

'Bang 'Bang 'Bang!! Leonard shot me in the stomach, right shoulder and head.

I lay powerless over the bullets that hit my body. Leonard was quite happy to be able to finish me off and saw blood flowing all over my body. He didn't feel the need to take too long to ensure my death because the three shots he fired were enough to make sure I died. One step, two steps Leonard away from me and wanted to leave the power plant area and he was immediately found surrounded by the police and an ambulance also came. He didn't expect his brother to immediately chase after him and Leonard dropped the gun he was holding.

"We found a man down, get him to the medics!" said Captain Brigss who was busy holding his brother in handcuffs.

"I won, bro. It won't be long until my government will release me and put a medal on my chest."

"Not with the crimes you've committed, Leo!"

"What are you saying?"

"Captain, we found this voice recorder in Grant's jacket."

"Good, that is a message Grant left to us."

"And proof from your own words, brother." The medics carried the motionless policeman to an ambulance and they left.

"Very impressive. I respected him for calling me to be killed to get my confession." Leonard was put in a police car.

"Do you want me to tell you something?"

"Anything else interesting?"

"You didn't kill Grant. You're just doing something pointless." The captain knocked on the roof of the car to take Leonard into custody. Leonard was still confused by his brother's last words earlier that he didn't succeed killing me.

"..." I felt that my head hurt a lot. Not only because of the sharp impact that stung my forehead, but also my stomach and shoulders.

"...ran.... Grant... re you... ten to me?" faint sound I hear and I try to open my eyes and use the nerves in my ears to hear more clearly.

"Grant, can you hear me?" I started to wake up from my stupor and saw Caith and Tess. Caith was patting my cheeks so I could recover quickly.

"Is this... heaven?"

"Too bad, welcome back," said Caith who had seen me awake with bandages on my head, shoulders and stomach.

"Hey... it's over, you can rest."

"How long did I... *ugh...!" I tried to get up from my bed and I felt a terrible pain in my head.

"Take it easy, Grant."

"So, I'm still alive."

"You dared to bring a device I haven't tested, Grant." Rip's voice rang in my ear.

"I said that the tool is ready."

"Is there someone who wants to explain to us?"

"Wait a moment." I'm still grinning from the pain in my head. Even if it was just a rubber bullet, it still gave me a concussion in my brain.

"Where do I start, huh..." we go back to when I made a new design for Rip's rubber bullets for him to make immediately. The new design is blood   paint.

I made the rubber bullet have a stock of blood red paint when it hits the target then the paint reservoir will break and color the target. At that time, I haven't tried it whether it works or not. In fact Leonard just let me go and he thought I was 'dead'."

"Where did you make those rubber bullets?"

"It was my project that I did because Captain Briggs asked me to."

"So it was a coincidence that he had rubber bullets."

"The next stage is more complicated. I asked Phill to track their movements."

"When did you do it?"

"I realized once I've been captured it won't take long for Leonard to put his plan into action to take me for whatever reason."

"He must have realized some of the mistakes he made when he planted the murders of Eugene and his kid and he believes I will be cleared of those charges as soon as possible."

"So, is that why you're rushing to get back to work?"

"Yes, I asked Phill to track their movements how they planned and I found one best point possible, namely at the power plant base and then I told Leonard about my escape."

"You told him?"

"How do you think he knew where I would be and tried to run away if it wasn't for me to tell him."

"Who else did you tell?"

"Phill, of course. He asked his man to shoot at the vehicle that was carrying me. Luckily I also survived that."

"The car shaking just made my head spin. When I got out of the car I could only stagger. That's where my plan is already running smoothly."

"Did Leonard not have his weapon with him?"

"I made the message to him. I need to talk one-on-one without weapons. He must have believed I got the gun from the officer who took me. He used that opportunity to take it from me without realizing that the gun from me was loaded with rubber bullets."

"Did he not hesitate to check the gun he stole before he used it?"

"I've already used that. He must have felt the heat in the gun."

"To whom?"

"One of the officers who tried to restrain me when the car overturned. I moved to get the gun faster than him."

"You got shot, how can he be sure that you're dead."

"Even it's a rubber bullet, if it hits you directly in the head it will knock you out of consciousness, Inspector. I had two gunshot pains in my stomach and shoulder. He still gets a chance to shoot one more time in the forehead."

"You 'die' once again, but this time I forgive you because you didn't lie to us."

"I think I've said enough. Can I come back... ow!"

"Relax, Grant. why are you in hurry?"

"I want to see Captain."

"Should I call him here?"

"It's about his brother."

"Stay in your bed and rest, Grant." Captain entered medical room. We are all surprised by his sudden appearance.

"I already know about Leo."

"What is it, Captain?" asked Eddie curiously.

"He not only failed to execute Grant, but also committed crimes in other countries."

"So, he has been exposed with his act of using defamation of the International Federal Bureau."

"What? They're just disguises?"

"I could tell at a glance that the federal police don't wear officer suits to arrest people. They're wearing tactical suits."

"I just realized that there is something strange about them."

"Thank you for being late for this, Inspector. I can be taken by them according to my plan."

"What do you mean? You think I'm better off not knowing anything?" they all laughed at Eddie's behavior trying to annoy me. Who would have thought that Eddie, who late of recognized the undercover agent, was also part of my plan.

They left me and went back to work except for Eddie who accompanied me at night. Opened the bandage Caith helped and there doesn't seem to be any problem at all on my forehead. I returned with Eddie who took me to the park and enjoyed the night breeze.

"Thank you," Eddie suddenly said to me out of nowhere.

"What was that for?"

"Well, for starters you're still alive."

"Of course I'm still alive, what are you talking about?"

"You shocked me when you muttered back then to be 'killed by Leonard'."

"It was just an analogy, Inspector, can't you tell the difference?"

"It's hard to tell when you're serious or just a parable."

"Thank you for worrying about me."

"Where does this caring come from? Not the usual you." He continued.

"But I feel very grateful."

"What is got into you today? Do I need to shoot the rubber bullet one more time at your forehead?"

"I think one time a day is enough, Inspector."

"Can you go home by yourself?"

"Of course, thanks for accompanying me all the way here."

"See you tomorrow." I walked over and looked at my cell phone. Phill sent a message saying thank you and congratulations on getting me out of trouble with Great Buturea. I only replied in moderation as a thank you for helping me and I only stayed at the hotel because my apartment was still closed by the police line.

———————END———————